WHERE DREAMS COME TRUE

VERVE
EDITIONS

PHOTOGRAPHS BY CAROLYN BROWN
ESSAY BY JIM DONOVAN
FOREWORD BY MAYOR LAURA MILLER

FOREWORD

I'll never forget the first time I saw Dallas as a college student in the mid-1970s. I saw smooth ribbons of road, perfectly manicured yards, tall glass buildings, a bustling downtown, all things shiny and new—it was truly the "Emerald City".

Our maverick history has seen Dallas transition from an economic center for agriculture and livestock, to the frontier of high-tech and business, fashion and entertainment, arts and music.

The spirit of Dallas is distinct—pretty much everything that happens here happens in a big way. Thinking big allows us to rewrite the rules, tame the untamed, and not only make dreams come true, but make the impossible possible.

Dallas is, once again, in the midst of a new beginning—a reawakening—a renaissance.

We are creating an overall cocktail of vibrancy that makes people from all over the globe want to be here with us. It begins with a robust, dynamic, 24/7 downtown. In addition to sports and live music, Dallas has more restaurants and shopping centers per capita than any other major U.S. city.

With a ground-breaking modern sculpture garden, a world-class symphony and art museum, and the largest collection of Art Deco buildings in the nation, Dallas is on its way to becoming the envy of the national arts community.

Our Trinity River Project is creating a park, wetlands and lakes roughly three times the size of New York City's Central Park. When complete, it will be the largest public works project in the history of our city, crowned by three spectacular signature bridges designed by internationally renowned architect, Santiago Calatrava.

I believe Dallas is upon its finest hour and fast becoming the most livable, vibrant and beautiful city in the nation. The road ahead leads us back to the "Emerald City" I saw as a young woman. Carolyn Brown's photographs and Jim Donovan's words beautifully capture the attitude, beauty and spirit of Dallas and clearly articulate our city pride and theme: "Live Large. Think Big."

I hope you will make this amazing book a centerpiece in your home and that you will always feel at home in Dallas.

Laura Miller, Mayor
Dallas, Texas

(PRECEDING SPREAD) DALLAS AND TRINITY RIVER. LIGHTS OF DALLAS CREATE A DREAM-LIKE VISION AS REFLECTED IN THE TRINITY RIVER. THE TRINITY FLOWS 423 MILES FROM THE CONFLUENCE OF THE ELM AND WEST FORKS TO THE COAST, MAKING IT THE LONGEST RIVER TO HAVE ITS ENTIRE COURSE IN TEXAS. (OPPOSITE) RENOWNED BRITISH SCULPTOR HENRY MOORE CREATED THIS MONUMENTAL SCULPTURE FOR CITY HALL PLAZA IN 1978. CALLED "THE DALLAS PIECE", IT IS 16 FEET HIGH, 24 FEET WIDE, AND WEIGHS 27,000 POUNDS. (FOLLOWING SPREAD) HALL OF STATE ENTRY. ALLIE TENNANT'S *GOLDEN TEJAS WARRIOR* AIMS HIS BOW TO THE SKY OVER THE ENTRANCE TO THE HALL OF STATE. THE DALLAS HISTORICAL SOCIETY MANAGES THE BUILDING, PRESENTING SPECIAL EXHIBITS AND PROGRAMS RELATING TO LOCAL AND STATE HISTORY AND MAKING ITS EXTENSIVE HISTORICAL ARCHIVES AVAILABLE TO RESEARCHERS.

History Architecture
Religion Urban Life
Arts Culture Medicine
Nature Education Business
Sports Plazas and Parks
Celebration

Where Dreams Come True

DALLAS PAST AND PRESENT

Carolyn Brown

John Neely Bryan stood on the bluff above the river. The sun was low and red, and the November wind was cool on his face. To the west the two streams became one, and the plains beyond were dotted with trees. No living thing moved within his sight. Only the water flowed slowly to the east, and it ran smooth and clear.

"Mi a ka—wash tay," he said, and turned to the Cherokee chief called Indian Ned.

"Here is the place we heard speak of, old friend.

The Land of the Three Forks—"

"Yes, I remember."

"It is a good place. We will return here to settle."

Bryan's gray pony, Neshoba, breathed noisily behind them.

The Indian's sorrel raised her head and whinnied, and the brown-and-white bear dog yawned.

Bryan shouldered his rifle, a faint smile playing on his lips.

Behind them a twig cracked. Bryan turned.

Six Cherokee stood not thirty feet away. At their head was the half-breed chief, Jesse Chisholm . . .

That was the beginning of Dallas, not a Larry McMurtry western. And almost every detail is true—Indian Ned, Neshoba, even the bear-hunting dog (named Tubby, after *tubbee*, a Choctaw word meaning "killer"). Jesse Chisholm, for whom the Chisholm Trail is named, was a good friend of Bryan's—fifteen years later Chisholm would provide sanctuary for Bryan after he shot a man who had insulted his wife.

The Three Forks area of Texas was Indian country long before Bryan came on the scene. Native Americans had fished its waters and hunted its deer, bear, and bison for at least forty thousand years. An ancient Indian village existed on today's Tenison Municipal Golf Course in present-day East Dallas. A "kill-site" for bison, used by Indians as long as five hundred years ago, was located on the eastern side of White Rock Lake, along with an extensive campsite at the lake's spillway. Most of these early residents were Caddo Indians, who settled along waterways in the Oklahoma-Arkansas-Texas triangle.

But there were no permanent residents of the area in early November of 1841 when Bryan left Holland Coffee's Trading Post on the Red River and ambled about one hundred miles down an Indian trail that is now Preston Road. He was an educated man, having attended college and studied law in his native Tennessee. He was also an experienced back-

(PRECEDING SPREAD) THE 179-FOOT-HIGH TRIANGULAR TOWER OF THE FEDERAL BUILDING MARKED THE GEOGRAPHIC CENTER OF THE TEXAS CENTENNIAL EXPOSITION. NOW KNOWN AS THE TOWER BUILDING, IT HAS RECENTLY BEEN RESTORED TO ITS 1936 GLORY. (THIS PAGE BELOW) COMMEMORATING THE CATTLE DRIVES THAT BROUGHT A MILLION CATTLE THROUGH DALLAS BEFORE THE CIVIL WAR. PIONEER PLAZA FEATURES NATIVE PLANTS, TREES, A FLOWING STREAM, AND 40 LARGER-THAN-LIFE BRONZE CATTLE, CREATED BY ROBERT SUMMERS OF GLEN ROSE, TEXAS. DEDICATED IN 1995 AND LOCATED JUST OUTSIDE THE DALLAS CONVENTION CENTER, PIONEER PLAZA QUICKLY BECAME ONE OF THE MOST VISITED TOURIST SITES IN DOWNTOWN DALLAS.

(ABOVE LEFT) FLAG AT "OLD RED". CONSTRUCTION OF DALLAS COUNTY'S SIXTH COURTHOUSE, AFFECTIONATELY KNOWN AS "OLD RED", BEGAN IN MARCH 1890, AND COUNTY OFFICIALS MOVED IN TWO YEARS LATER. BUILT OF PECOS SANDSTONE AND ARKANSAS GRANITE IN THE EXUBERANT ROMANESQUE-REVIVAL STYLE POPULAR AT THE TIME, THE COURTHOUSE ORIGINALLY BOASTED A 90-FOOT CLOCK TOWER, SCHEDULED TO BE REBUILT IN 2005 AS PART OF AN OVERALL RESTORATION OF THE HISTORIC STRUCTURE. (ABOVE RIGHT) MAIN STREET IN OLD CITY PARK. LOCATED IN DALLAS, OLDEST PUBLIC PARK (CREATED IN 1876), OLD CITY PARK: THE HISTORICAL VILLAGE OF DALLAS IS A COLLECTION OF 38 HISTORIC STRUCTURES FROM THROUGHOUT NORTH CENTRAL TEXAS REFLECTING THE ARCHITECTURAL AND CULTURAL HERITAGE OF THE REGION BETWEEN 1840 AND 1910. THE SIMPLE SHOPS ALONG THE BRICK-PAVED MAIN STREET STAND IN DRAMATIC CONTRAST TO THE MODERN SKYSCRAPERS VISIBLE IN THE BACKGROUND. (BELOW) WILSON BLOCK. IN 1899 HENRIETTA FRICHOT WILSON AND HER HUSBAND FREDERICK WILSON BUILT A BEAUTIFUL VICTORIAN HOME ON SWISS AVENUE FOR THEMSELVES AND THEIR TWO CHILDREN. THEY HAD ACQUIRED AN ENTIRE CITY BLOCK IN EAST DALLAS FROM HENRIETTA'S UNCLE JACOB NUSSBAUMER, A SETTLER FROM THE ILL-FATED LA RÉUNION COLONY. THE WILSONS BUILT SIX MORE HOUSES ON THEIR LAND, WHICH GAVE THEM THE OPPORTUNITY TO SELECT THEIR NEIGHBORS.

woodsman who spoke seven Indian dialects and had many Indian friends. By the time he returned to Three Forks, the old Indian chief, Ned, had died. But Bryan brought two horses, a dog, and five other frontiersmen who stayed long enough to help erect a shelter and then lit out for greener pastures. And he brought a dream.

It was not by chance that he decided on that particular spot on the river, which was known even then as the Trinity. He knew it had the shallowest and best natural ford for many miles. He was also confident that the Trinity would prove navigable. His goal was to found a settlement, and he believed that these natural assets could one day make it a major trading center.

Bryan and his friends set up camp—a ramshackle hut of poles, brush, and mud—on a bluff overlooking the river, just

BECAUSE IRIS SMITH, OWNER OF OAK CLIFF FLORAL, LOVES IRISES, ARTIST CARLOS NICHOLLS INCLUDED THEM IN THIS COLORFUL MURAL ON HER BUILDING. HE ALSO INCORPORATED EXISTING ELEMENTS, SUCH AS THE AIR CONDITIONER AND SHRUBBERY, TO CREATE A DELIGHTFUL EXAMPLE OF VERNACULAR ART.

about where Main Street goes under the Triple Underpass in Dallas today (The river was diverted a mile west in 1928). Soon he began a primitive trading post; his first customers were the peaceful Caddo Indians. He then staked a claim to the 640 acres that were lawfully his. The Republic of Texas was then a young nation eager to attract new homesteaders to North Texas. It established a national road (beginning in Bastrop, below Austin, and running north to the Red River), and protected it with eight forts and fifteen Ranger companies. In addition, the promotional efforts of the Peters Colony, a Texas-approved company that sold land in this virgin wilderness, attracted many pioneers from the western states of Kentucky, Illinois, Tennessee, and Missouri. As the settlers arrived, Bryan surveyed and platted his township and began

Dallas' first bicycle was purchased by Hugh Blakeney in 1876. It had wooden wheels (a large one in the front and a smaller one in the back) and iron tires. Six years later Dallasite Groos Scruggs paid $162.50 for the first bicycle in town with rubber tires.

selling lots to them (newlyweds got one free). Within a year there were several families in the small town that Bryan dubbed "Dallas", probably after Commodore Alexander James Dallas, a well-known naval hero of the War of 1812.

Soon Bryan was also operating a ferry across the Trinity. For several years the little hamlet had more visitors than permanent residents. But European emigrants, including many well-educated Swiss, Belgian, and French people involved in the idealistic, but ill-fated, La Réunion utopian colony to the west, soon joined the town. They helped lay the foundations for many of Dallas' important cultural institutions.

The life of Dallas' colorful founder reads like several Louis L'Amour novels rolled into one. When Bryan wasn't tending to the full-time job of making his young town work, he served as a go-between for Sam Houston, then president of Texas, in peace negotiations with the Indians. He took off (with every other man in town except one) for the California Gold Rush; he returned a year later, unsuccessful. He served for years as a captain in the Texas Rangers, chasing outlaws and renegades. At the ripe old age of fifty, he enlisted in the Texas cavalry to fight in the Civil War.

In 1852, Bryan sold his holdings in Dallas to Alexander Cockrell, a close friend and businessman, for seven thousand dol-

(LEFT) VIRGEN LAW. VERNACULAR ART ENLIVENS THE WALL OF A LAW OFFICE IN THE BISHOP ARTS DISTRICT, RECALLING THE COLORFUL PAINTED FACADES IN MEXICO. (RIGHT) CASITA LUPE CAFE. THE CAFE IN OAK CLIFF BEGAN LIFE IN THE 1930S AS A POLAR BEAR ICE CREAM PARLOR.

lars. Bryan's personal life spiraled downward from there—assisted by good friend John Barleycorn. He died in 1877 in the State Lunatic Asylum in Austin, six months after he was admitted for "intemperance". No one knows where he is buried.

Bryan's dream of Dallas as a great port city, and thus a center of trade, never materialized. A local entrepreneur built a flatboat in 1852, loaded it with cotton bales, and started downstream bound for Houston. Four months later he had only gone seventy miles. Then the river became too low, the cotton was shipped to its destination by wagon. In 1868, the only steamboat to make the journey up the unpredictable Trinity from Galveston took a year and four days—an unacceptable delivery time, even before Federal Express began offering next-day service. But when some Dallas businessmen formed the Trinity River Navigation Company in 1892 and their steamship, the *Harvey,* arrived the next year, the celebration was even bigger than the one that had greeted the railroad two decades earlier. The *Harvey* operated as a pleasure boat over the next five years, running day trips to McCommas Bluff. By 1898, the boat was sold. But hard-headed dreamers continued to sink money into Trinity improvement, and it's only been over the last half-century that the idea of a navigable river has faded away.

Bryan's successor as Dallas' #1 citizen, Alexander Cockrell, was a man of boundless energy. Within a few years he had built a sawmill, a general store, and a sturdy bridge over the Trinity that brought a steady flow of travelers and nearby settlers. Dallas was growing, and Cockrell was its chief architect. But he was shot to death in 1858, when the town marshal emptied eight bullets into his abdomen in a dispute over money. He left his thirty-eight year old wife and mother of four, Sarah Horton Cockrell. She quickly assumed control of her husband's assets and became the town's leading entrepreneur, often listing men as the heads of her businesses in those pre-suffragist days. For fourteen years she owned the ferry once owned by Bryan; she developed three of the town's finest hotels; she led the fight to get the first iron bridge built over the Trinity; she was the dominant partner in the first flour mill; and she owned a considerable amount of downtown property. She was Dallas' first great businesswoman and first millionaire. When she died in 1892, Dallas was the most populous city in Texas. The city directory listed her occupation as "capitalist".

How did a town that had no viable outlet to the sea, no mineral resources, little fertile land, and poor access become the signature city of Texas? Because its farsighted, determined citizens wanted it that way—and then made it happen. Like this:

In 1850, they won two close elections that made Dallas a permanent county seat—mainly due to Bryan's offer to donate

UNION STATION. THE CONSTRUCTION OF A NEW PASSENGER STATION IN 1916 CONSOLIDATED FIVE PREVIOUS TERMINALS USED BY NINE RAIL-ROAD LINES SERVING DALLAS. DESIGNED BY CHICAGO ARCHITECT JARVIS HUNT IN THE BEAUX-ARTS STYLE, IT COST $5 MILLION, THE COSTLI-EST BUILDING IN DALLAS TO THAT TIME.

land for a courthouse square. As the area's center of government, Dallas gained considerable status.

In 1872, the city offered five thousand dollars, 115 acres of land, and a free right of way to the north-south Houston & Texas Central (H&TC). The offer brought the first railroad in the state steaming through Dallas. A year later, they got the state legislature to require that the transcontinental Texas & Pacific (T&P) cross the H&TC "within one mile" of Browder Springs—the source of Dallas' water. Not satisfied with having the T&P merely nearby, the townspeople went further. They voted 192-0 to offer the T&P $100,000 and a right of way, bringing the railroad right through downtown. The railroads made Dallas a key distribution center for the entire Southwest, and helped develop the wealth of cotton and grain resources found in the blackland prairies surrounding it.

In 1912, the townspeople lobbied to bring a Federal Reserve Bank to Dallas. Though competing with several larger cities, they won, establishing Dallas as a secure financial center.

In 1936, they went after another big prize—the Texas Centennial Exposition. Their by now well-honed powers of persuasion (plus an offer of ten million dollars, 242 acres of land, and many buildings, museums, and other cultural facilities) made them winners again. Over the next two years, thirteen million visitors and the millions of dollars of revenue they generated virtually pulled the city out of the Depression. And Dallas became *the* major city in Texas—though it hadn't even existed a hundred years earlier.

Today Dallas continues to reflect its "make it happen" history. The city's still a mecca for entrepreneurs, speculators, developers, and hucksters—in short, for every kind of dreamer alive. Those who have seen their dreams come true include Roger Horchow, the mail-order mogul; Stanley Marcus and family, retailers *par excellence*; Bette Graham, inventor of Liquid Paper; Kenneth Cooper, the aerobics pioneer; Robert Crandall, the American Airlines steersman; Ebby Halliday, one of the most successful realtors in America; H. L. Hunt, the gambling oilman who at one time was called "the world's richest man"; his son, Lamar Hunt, the founder of the American Football League and the Super Bowl; Mary

(LEFT AND RIGHT) ART DECO DETAILS. DOWNTOWN DALLAS REMAINS RICH IN ARCHITECTURAL DETAILS VISIBLE TO THOSE WHO TAKE THE TIME TO LOOK. THE FORMER HEADQUARTERS OF LONE STAR GAS ON HARWOOD STREET, CONSTRUCTED IN 1931, SPORTS ART DECO PANELS. (CENTER) THE VILLAGE THEATER OPENED IN 1935 AS THE FIRST LUXURY SUBURBAN MOVIE THEATER IN TEXAS. IT ANCHORED THE NEW HIGHLAND PARK SHOPPING CENTER, AMERICA'S FIRST PLANNED SHOPPING CENTER WHERE THE STORES FACE INWARD WITH PARKING IN THE CENTER AND A UNIFIED ARCHITECTURAL STYLE. THE THEATER HAS BEEN REMODELED AS A SMALL MULTIPLEX CINEMA SHOWING FIRST-RUN FILMS.

Kay Ash, the cosmetics queen; J. M. Haggar, the world's largest manufacturer of dress slacks; Trammell Crow, the nation's most successful real estate developer; and of course H. Ross Perot, the former IBM salesman turned millionaire and presidential candidate. And don't forget Barney, the world's most popular dinosaur, who lives in Dallas when he's not on the road entertaining his millions of pre-MTV fans.

Big D has come a long way from the single shack of poles and mud built by John Neely Bryan. Now the seventh-largest city in the nation, Dallas is known for its upscale department stores and malls. It has more shopping centers and more retail space per capita than any other U.S. city, and the Dallas Market Center is the world's largest wholesale merchandise mart. As longtime Texas historian A. C. Greene pointed out, "Dallas has always been a city with its excuse for being that 'you can get it there'"—and you still can. Dallas offers four massive malls (Northpark, the Galleria, Valley View, and Prestonwood) along with smaller malls and shopping centers (the Crescent, Highland Park Village, Uptown's West Village). Loaded with every kind of retail outlet imaginable, they celebrate the city's patron saints of shopping, the Sanger brothers. Lehman and Philip Sanger arrived in Dallas with the railroads after the Civil War, and revolutionized mercantile marketing in the Southwest. Their influence is still felt; Herbert Marcus worked for them, and Roger Horchow worked for Neiman Marcus.

Dallas issued its first traffic ticket in 1885. The offense was driving a horse too fast on Main Street; the fine was one dollar. In 1900, the city's first auto speeder, Erle Freeman, was arrested for driving ten miles per hour.

You can certainly get sports here, too. Dallas is a sports-mad city in every way. The city boasts competitive, big league teams in every major sport: the Mavericks (basketball), the Sidekicks (indoor soccer), the Burn (soccer), the Stars (hockey), and the nearby Texas Rangers (baseball). Perhaps the best-known of the teams is the Dallas Cowboys, who have a stadium with a hole in the roof so God can watch His favorite football team. It seems that most Dallas residents eagerly watch games, compete in them, or work out in some low- or high-impact fashion. (They look good doing it, too.)

And Dallas continues to welcome new businesses with open arms. In fact, the Dallas-Fort Worth area is the country's third-fastest-growing job market, just behind Atlanta and Chicago. The city's financial dependence on oil production and petroleum-based products has decreased in recent years as the local economy has embraced a number of other industries, including aeronautics, meat packing, fashion, cotton goods, printing and publishing, electronics, and advertising. Only two other cities in the country headquarter more Fortune 500 companies. Dallas is still one of the nation's most important centers of finance and banking. Thus, Dallas has emerged from the recession in Texas during the eighties as a stronger city, a city of diversity.

That's diversity with a big D. Dallas has many faces, and they are all open and inviting. Dallas is exactly what it appears to be—a city that rewards hard work and confidence, a city that congratulates ambition and success.

And Dallas knows how to celebrate that success. It knows how to have a good time, with plenty of places to do it. A good spot to start is the West End, a collection of old, downtown warehouses. Farsighted developers began a decade ago to transform them into a variety of popular restaurants, bars, shops, and offices. The area is now one of the first destinations on the list of any visitors who want to see the city's sights. On the other end of town, the funky neighborhood of Deep Ellum offers a Soho-like combination of artists' lofts, hip nightclubs, and hipper shops and art galleries. Deep Ellum began as a Black Freedman's Town built after the Civil War, and the thriving neighborhood was later home to musicians such as Blind Lemon Jefferson and Leadbelly (Huddie Ledbetter). It then fell into disuse following the building of Central Expressway a half-century ago. Two decades ago, a new generation of musicians, artists, and gallery owners began to reclaim it. Its considerable popularity now almost threatens to subvert the fresh independence that defines its allure.

Many people are drawn to the nightclubs along lower Greenville Avenue, which runs north from just above downtown; until a decade or so ago the stretch north of Mockingbird Lane was home to bigger and louder nightspots, but many of those have disappeared. Just across Central Expressway at Mockingbird lies Southern Methodist University, the city's center of higher learning since it was founded in 1910. Restaurant Row, in far northwest Dallas, is a conglomeration of large, upscale chain restaurants and clubs whose neon signs and size make this strip a little Las Vegas. These areas and others—Uptown (McKinney Avenue and the surrounding area just north of downtown); Addison's Belt Line Road, in far North Dallas; Cedar Springs and Lemmon avenues in Oak Lawn—give Dallas a diversity in cuisine, music, arts, and entertainment equaled in few other cities.

Balancing the conspicuous consumption and night life of Dallas is a strong religious spirit. New York's borough of Brooklyn was called "the City of Churches" in the nineteenth century, but Dallas rivals that reputation today with its 1,300 churches and temples (It's been known as the "Buckle of the Bible Belt" for quite some time). Religion here is a pervasive presence. Billboards advertise competing churches, and prayer invocations are given before many large, public gatherings. Big D is home to the largest Episcopalian, Presbyterian, and Southern Baptist congregations in the country; two of the top ten best-attended Methodist churches are here. Though the city is largely Protestant, a wide variety of religions flourish here, in large Catholic and Jewish congregations as well as in smaller but growing immigrant groups of Buddhist, Muslim, Baha'i, and many others. There is even a lovely Hare Krishna temple in East Dallas whose income is supplemented by the excellent vegetarian restaurant next door.

The self-congratulatory style of Dallas can inspire jealous rages in many Texans outside the city. But they put these aside when it's time for the Texas State Fair. It began as a popular county fair in 1859, and became the official Texas State Fair in 1886. At the turn of the century the fair's site, Fair Park, was open year-round. Like a sprawling Coney Island, Fair Park boasted a Scenic Railway, Amusement Row (today's Midway), and irresistible entertainments like "Shoot the Chutes" and "The Tickler". But it was not until the Texas Centennial Exposition of 1936 that today's fabulous collection of Art Deco buildings and the Cotton Bowl were constructed at the park. Though many of its attractions are open all year, Fair Park draws its largest crowds when the State Fair is held annually in October. The fair's famous symbol, Big Tex, has greeted fairgoers since 1952. He's a larger-than-life cowboy who wears size seventy boots and a seventy-five-gallon hat.

(ABOVE LEFT) FIRST BAPTIST CHURCH WAS BUILT IN 1890, HAVING A SANCTUARY OF AMERICA'S LARGEST BAPTIST CONGREGATION, IT IS DOWN-TOWN'S FINEST REMAINING VICTORIAN-ERA STRUCTURE, COMBINING GOTHIC REVIVAL AND ROMANESQUE DETAILS. (ABOVE RIGHT) DEEP IN DEEP ELLUM, COLORFUL MURALS BY LOCAL ARTISTS DECORATE THE HISTORIC GOOD LATIMER TUNNEL. NEXT TO DOWNTOWN, IT FEATURES LOFT LIVING AND RICH NIGHTLIFE. "ELLUM" IS A 1930S COLLOQUIALISM OF "ELM", ONE OF THE PRIME STREETS THAT RUNS THROUGH THE AREA.

What, if anything, do other major cities have that Dallas *doesn't* have? Let's see now:

Mountains—There's nothing resembling mountains near Dallas. That's why we keep Colorado open twenty-four hours a day—especially during skiing season.

Coastline/Beach—Two lovely lakes lie within the city limits (White Rock and the smaller Bachman) and a brace of them surround the city (almost every one built by the Army Corps of Engineers). Dallas has no ocean coast nearby, so if the lakes aren't enough, there's always one of the area's massive waterparks.

Winter—Does Dallas have winter? Technically, yes. Effectively, no. If winter's so great, how do you account for all the snowbirds from points north? They talk about leaves turning red—until their skin turns blue.

"Great" Earthquakes, Famines, Fires, Floods, Blackouts, Hurricanes, Riots, and Other Disasters—Historic moments we can do without, thank you. A large fire burned most of the Dallas business district in 1860, but the city's population was only about five hundred then. The fire had a positive effect: It forced residents to begin building with more fire-resistant materials, and in no time the town was stronger than ever. There was a serious flood in 1908 which resulted in five deaths and $2.5 million in property damage, but "Great" doesn't apply.

Dallas is a young city, just over a century and a half old. Like many other large American cities, it struggles with crime, unemployment, transportation, housing, education, and growth—challenges that must be addressed. But Dallas' traditions of farsighted planning and bold initiative have helped the city triumph over any number of problems. The failure of the Trinity as a navigable river was an early blow, but it forced Dallas citizens to look to the railroads to satisfy their access needs. The flood of 1908 resulted in the adoption of the 1911 Kessler Plan, which moved the river a mile west. The downtown fire of 1860 and the tragic assassination of President Kennedy a century later also tested the city's mettle. These and many other moments of crisis have, in the end, made Dallas stronger and better. The city's great-hearted people, both civic leaders and private citizens, will do the same in the future. Dallas will undoubtedly meet the challenges of the future with equal courage and aplomb. And Dallas will continue to be a place where dreamers can make something of themselves—a place where dreams come true.

ARCHITECTURE OF DALLAS Richard R. Brettell Ph.D.

Many great American cities started as tiny places with immense dreams. In fact, the western half of the United States is littered with small towns—and even ghost towns—founded with the idea that, within decades, they would be world-class cities. Dallas is one of the few success stories. With a straggling, sometimes dry, river and two crossing railroad lines on the almost completely flat plains of North Texas, its site did not inspire confidence in the decades after the Civil War when it claimed regional attention. Yet, a century later, it was among the most vibrant cities in America, with a burgeoning architectural culture that continues to make its mark felt on both the nation and the larger world.

It is safe to say that, in spite of admirable office towers, dignified civic buildings, grand houses, and creditable schools, there was not a single building of national importance in Dallas until the opening in 1915 of Dallas Hall at Southern Methodist University. Designed by the venerable Boston architectural firm of Shepley, Rutan, and Coolidge (the oldest architecture firm in America), it was modeled on Thomas Jefferson's library for the University of Virginia and, of course, on its source, Hadrian's Pantheon in Rome. It made a claim for national and international attention, recalling the great library building for Columbia University by McKim, Meade, and White and the recently completed campus for MIT by

William Welles Bosworth in Cambridge. Dallas Hall asserted Dallas' ambitions and, although it sits in University Park, was paid for by a public subscription of the people of Dallas.

Dallas Hall happened because the leadership of Dallas had decided to create an important Master Plan by the Kansas City and St. Louis planner, George E. Kessler. Published in 1912 and slowly put into place during the succeeding two decades, this plan created the curving parks and boulevards in Oak Cliff that bear his name as well as the nationally known Turtle Creek Park. Others too, joined this trend toward "City Beautiful Planning" with the founding of Swiss Avenue and Highland Park even before World War I deflected Dallas from its own development and plugged it into world affairs.

The 1920s saw an upsurge in the city's population and the arrival of several architects who began to reshape the city to its national and international dreams. The first of these was a young Texan named Mark Lemmon, who arrived after architecture school at MIT, service in World War I in France, and a year with a major architectural firm in New York. Lemmon became the presiding architect of historical Dallas, and his homes, schools, churches, university buildings, and even public houses gave the Dallas metropolis the look of a solid, traditional city. Whether Romanesque, Gothic, Jacobean, Georgian, or Moderne, his buildings plugged Dallas into the traditional civilizations of Europe, even as its own government was being polluted by the Ku Klux Klan.

Interestingly, the elites of Dallas who were patrons of its best architects were those who fought the pernicious politics that dominated the city in that decade. Dallas didn't really get "Modern" until 1935, when it began its long battle with the city of Fort Worth for the Texas Centennial Exhibition.

Opened to great acclaim in 1936 at the height of a national depression, the complex of Art Deco or "Moderne" buildings created at Fair Park for the Texas Centennial remains to this day a masterpiece. Often called the largest complex of Art Deco buildings in America, it certainly is among the very finest, and now that its sculpture, paintings, and fountains have been restored, it looks every bit as grand in 2005 as it did in 1936. What is interesting about this complex is that it resulted from a true collaboration of Dallas artists and architects with their counterparts from across the state and nation. The consulting architect, Paul Cret, was a Philadelphian who was creating a master plan for the campus of the University of Texas at Austin, and the major coordinating architect was another Dallas architect, George Dahl, who came to Dallas

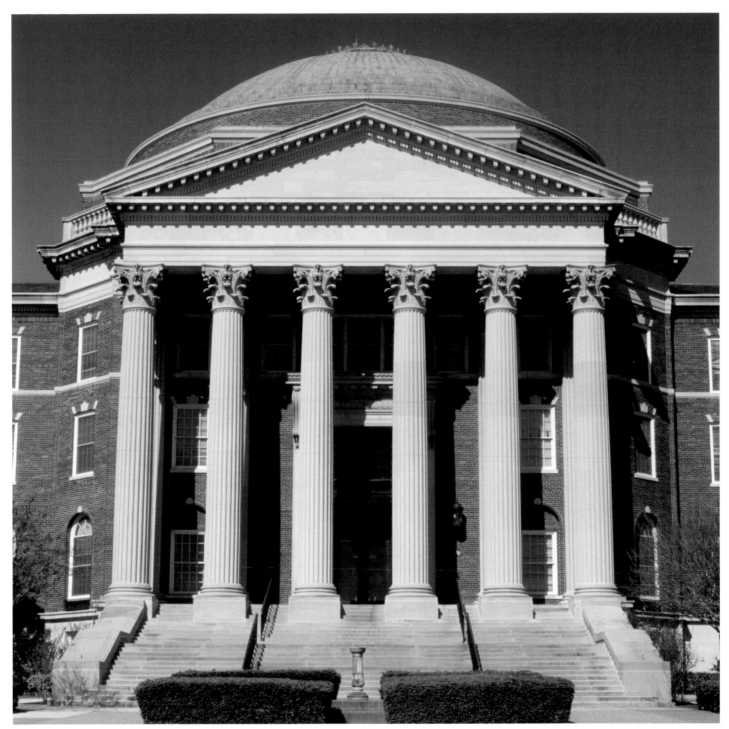

(OPPOSITE) ALTHOUGH NOT NATIVE TO DALLAS, AZALEAS GAINED INSTANT POPULARITY WHEN THEY WERE INTRODUCED FOLLOWING WORLD WAR II. THEIR VIVID COLORS ATTRACT SIGHTSEERS TO LAKESIDE DRIVE IN HIGHLAND PARK, TURTLE CREEK, AND PARKS THROUGH-OUT THE AREA. (ABOVE) FOUNDED IN 1911, SOUTHERN METHODIST UNIVERSITY FULFILLED THE DREAMS OF DALLAS LEADERS FOR AN INSTITUTION OF HIGHER LEARNING. BECAUSE LOCAL RESIDENTS DONATED THE FUNDS TO BUILD THE CENTERPIECE OF THE CAMPUS, A DOMED STRUCTURE INSPIRED BY THOMAS JEFFERSON'S ROTUNDA AT THE UNIVERSITY OF VIRGINIA, IT WAS NAMED DALLAS HALL.

from Minnesota via MIT and remained one of the most important figures in the city's architectural history.

Three other important regional architects arrived in Dallas in the late '20s and early '30s and made a major impact on the city. The earliest of these was David Williams, the designer of Greenway Parks, one of the first planned communities in the city, and the creator, with his younger colleague, O'Neil Ford, of a new kind of vernacular Texas modernism. These two men combed the state for eighteenth and nineteenth century buildings that had withstood the harsh climate and cultural upheavals of this vast state. They worked to invent from these sources a kind of handmade vernacular modernism that remains to this day a defining characteristic of Dallas Style. Perhaps the finest work of this type is the Williams (no relation) House on McFarlin in Highland Park. The third of these figures was a New Yorker named Howard Meyer, who came to Dallas in 1931 with an architectural degree from Columbia University and experience with Le Corbusier in France and Frank Lloyd Wright in his New York period of the late '20s. Indeed, by 1931 Dallas had five major architects with national experience and reputations working to define the city.

If the "public works" projects of the Depression created Fair Park and added to the Kessler legacy with other corporative ventures, it was not really until the conclusion of World War II and the defiant technological dominance of the United States that Dallas really took off. Indeed, oil and air-conditioning were to be the two factors that pushed Dallas into its place in the national scene. With the arrival of a group of MIT engineers in Dallas and the eventual creation of Texas Instruments, and with the extraordinary progress in the concrete business of Texas Industries along with the national attention on Dallas Style led by the indomitable Stanley Marcus of Neiman Marcus, Dallas entered the consciousness of

America with its own architectural ambitions. Another young Texan, Bud Oglesby, arrived in the city from training in Cambridge and Finland in the late '40s, and Texas Instruments gave incredible work to O'Neil Ford and his architectural friends from Mexico and the western United States. All of these factors created the conditions for a ruthlessly driven belief in the future of Dallas and in its importance in the United States and the world. Major real estate developers worked to lure corporations, conventions, trade fairs, and national associations to Dallas, and a building boom completely unprecedented in the history of the city began at the conclusion of World War II.

Since then, architecture has been the dominant art form of this ambitious city. The late '50s saw the building of the only surviving theater by Frank Lloyd Wright on Turtle Creek. Then the architectural floodgates opened. A triumphantly modernist City Hall built by the young I.M. Pei and an international airport complex the size of Manhattan by St. Louis' Helmut, Obata, Kassebaum were the legacy of Texas Instrument executive J. Erik Jonsson, who was mayor of the city. And these created the conditions for an art museum by Edward Larrabee Barnes; office towers by Philip Johnson, Paul Rudolphe, I.M.

Pei, Harry Cobb, Skidmore, Owings and Merrill, Eraldo Cassuta, Welton Beckett, and others; a symphony hall by I.M. Pei; a shopping center by Eero Saarinen and Kevin Roche; a department store and an urban garden by Philip Johnson; and major private homes by Frank Lloyd Wright, Edward Durrell Stone, Philip Johnson, Richard Meier, Antoine Predock, and Stephen Holl. This is the stuff of raw architectural ambition, and few other American cities between the coasts (perhaps only Chicago and Houston) can boast such a stellar list of nationally significant buildings.

Dallas architects also made extraordinary contributions to the city during these same decades, although none of them received the plum commissions. Meyer's 3525 Turtle Creek Boulevard is among the finest modernist apartment towers from '50s America, and his Temple Emanu-El was on the cover of *Life* magazine when it opened in 1957 to house the largest Jewish congregation in America. It is surely, architecturally, the finest sacred space in the city. For O'Neil Ford there was the complex for Texas Instruments with his friend, the great Mexican architect-engineer, Felix Candela, and homes for three of its four founding partners. Bud Oglesby built wonderful buildings for education (the McDermott Library at University of Texas at Dallas), medical research, corporate offices, and multi-family and single-family residence. Local architects George Dahl and Harwood K. Smith created two of the largest architectural offices in the country in Dallas after World War II. Their buildings for large corporations can be found from Boston to Seattle.

Since the 1980s, Dallas has seen several boom and bust real estate cycles with alternating faith and disbelief in the

(ABOVE) TOWER PETROLEUM, DESIGNED BY ARCHITECT MARK LEMMON, IS ONE OF THE FEW ZIG-ZAG MODERNE STYLED BUILDINGS LEFT IN DOWNTOWN DALLAS. IT IS 23 STORIES TALL, WITH AN OVERALL HEIGHT OF 315 FEET, MAKING IT THE 45TH TALLEST BUILDING IN THE CITY. (PHOTO: COURTESY MEADOWS MUSEUM)

power of architecture. The suburbs have grown with phenomenal energy, and large American corporations that have moved to the metroplex have, by and large, avoided the city of Dallas itself. The architecture of corporate, suburban Dallas has not been inspired, and the immense corporate campuses for such giants as Exxon-Mobil, J.C. Penney, Nortel, and EDS are more interesting for sheer scale than for architectural imagination. The sole suburban exception is the extraordinary development called Solana, north of the DFW airport. This complex of buildings developed by the Los Angeles real estate firm of McGuire-Thomas was designed for IBM by Ricardo Legoretta from Mexico City and Mitchell-Giurgula from Philadelphia. Set in a wonderfully hilly oak forest with native planting and water systems, these walled compounds set a standard that one only hopes Dallas and other cities will follow.

There are perhaps two important trends in early twenty-first-century Dallas. The first concerns urban and suburban infill with literally hundreds of mixed-use complexes in the center city and of new suburbs designed according to the people-friendly and fundamentally anti-modernist principals of "The New Urbanism." New "downtowns" have sprung up in northern suburbs such as Addison, Plano, and Frisco and a major mixed-use land development planned by the Billingsley Company for a large ranch north of DallLionel Morrison are the most notable. Interestingly, the latter is decid-

edly modernist, following the model of Solana, but without the regionalist character of Legoretta's architecture. The new suburban downtowns, like the infill architecture in and around downtown Dallas itself, have been dominated by thoroughly pleasant "lite-modern" or "Mediterranean" architecture. No adventure there. Yet, central Dallas has made real advances in modernist multi-family housing, following the example set in the 1950s and '60s by Bud Oglesby. With superb buildings by local architects Gary Cunningham, Edward Baum, Lionel Morrison, Thomas Krehenbuhl, Russell Buchanan, and others, the townhouse and multifamily urban development in Dallas is of national significance.

It is, however, with the architecture of the arts and culture that Dallas is making its greatest play for international approval at the dawn of the new century. The Italian Renzo Piano was the earliest of the European architects to make a mark on Dallas with his superbly detailed and technologi-

cally sophisticated building for the Nasher Sculpture Center. This building and garden occupy an entire block in the Dallas Arts District, and their completion heralded a renaissance for that district. Within five years, the Winspear Opera House will be completed to the design of the distinguished British architect, Sir Norman Foster. And the experimentally edgy Rotterdam firm of Metropolitan Architects, dominated by its chief designer, Rem Koolhaas, has designed the performing arts center in the district. Allied Architects of Portland, Oregon, will design the new building for the Arts Magnet High School, and there has been much talk of hiring the legendary Frank Gehry to design a new Museum of Natural History for Dallas in a larger undeveloped site at the edge of the city. Like many great provincial cities, Dallas has succeeded better at spending serious money hiring national and international architects to build its local buildings than at creating it designers. Thus, it has been accused by New York critics of "consuming rather than producing culture". Yet, a vibrant architectural scene has developed in the city with the growth of the Dallas Architecture Forum, the Dallas Architecture Foundation, Preservation Dallas, and the architecture school at the University of Texas at Arlington. It is true, to say that, outside the cities of New York, Chicago, and Los Angeles, there has been no architectural community of international standards developed in the United States. Yet, with its roots firmly planted and its ambitions set uniformly high, Dallas, together with its greatest rival, Houston, is in position to create such a community.

(ABOVE) MEXICAN ARCHITECT RICARDO LEGORETTA'S COLORFUL SOLANA OFFICE COMPLEX AT SOUTH LAKE IS AN IMPORTANT CONTRIBUTION TO MODERN DESIGN IN THE REGION.

Urban Dallas

PEGASUS Gail Thomas, Ph. D

For those of us who have lived for a while in Dallas, Pegasus is more than the myth of the winged horse. Pegasus is Dallas' image, its own symbol, a sign of Dallas' spirit. It is always there, brazen-red in the sun and illumined in the sky at night. What power an image has! Pegasus has been our Eiffel Tower, our Golden Gate Bridge, our Big Ben. Growing up in McKinney, I remember coming into the city by way of Greenville Avenue, eager for the first glimpse of the Flying Red Horse. Stanley Marcus once told me that when he was flying home from travels, he would walk into the Braniff cockpit to join the pilots as they made their approach to Dallas so that he would be the first to see the revolving red glowing horse.

The Dallas Pegasus is the largest Pegasus in the world. It is thirty by forty feet and weighs almost fifteen tons. It flies four hundred feet above street level. The Flying Red Horse was added to the top of the Magnolia Building in 1934, twelve years after the construction of the home office of the Magnolia Petroleum Company, the tallest building south of Washington, D.C. when it was erected in 1922, and a source of great civic pride.

People in Dallas are still protective of our Pegasus. In 1979 there was a fear about what would happen to the sacred horse when news came that the City had sold the Magnolia Building to a San Francisco developer. When the new owner was called and asked about the future of our winged horse, he replied, "Don't worry. Pegasus is immortal. It cannot be destroyed". What actually happened was that the City had sold the building, but retained ownership of the Flying Red Horse. City Hall had cleverly planned to guarantee that Pegasus will fly in Dallas as long as the building stands.

The Pegasus story is a universal one, originating in Greek legends of a magnificent winged horse who sprang from the neck of the Medusa, a serpent-haired Gorgon whose single gaze could turn one to stone. It takes a bold act to cut off the head of the Medusa, an act the hero Perseus performs to release Pegasus, who transforms adversity into new opportunity. Pegasus creates the spring Hippocrene on Mount Helicon with a stamp of his hoof. This spring is the meeting place of the Muses, the sources of poetic inspiration. Pegasus was tamed by Bellerophon and thereafter carried the young hero to perform great exploits. But when Bellerophon, with overweening pride, attempted to ride Pegasus to Olympus to join the

(PRECEDING SPREAD) HYATT PANORAMA AT DUSK.
MAKING A COMPLETE REVOLUTION EVERY 55 MINUTES,
THE BALL ATOP REUNION TOWER PROVIDES ONE OF
THE MOST DRAMATIC VIEWS OF DALLAS. (LEFT) THREE
BRONZE COWBOYS RIDE HERD ON THE CATTLE

gods, Pegasus threw him back to earth. Pegasus reigns today in the heavens as a constellation.

In 1994, the city dedicated Pegasus Plaza, at the foot of the Magnolia Building, in commemoration of Pegasus as the spirit of Dallas. Knowing that there are two fresh water springs under the basement of the Magnolia Building, and that during past times of severe drought these springs served as a source of drinking water, the designers of the plaza constructed two springs within the park design. One spring bubbles up within the mist fountain in the plaza and at its base is this inscription: "Where the hoof of Pegasus hits the ground a well springs forth and the muses come to dance and sing." Scattered throughout the plaza are enormous muse stones telling the story of the nine muses, and how, when they come, they bring with them life and culture.

The 2000 Millennium project for Dallas consisted of restoring the rusted, and no longer revolving, Flying Red Horse. Regrettably, the horse had not turned in over twenty years; this icon of the city had grown dark. Swaying in the wind from loosened support braces, the neon tubing that formerly glowed red in the night sky had broken; the ball-bearing, rotating base was rusted and still. The beacon, so familiar to visitors and citizens alike, had gone out. The call went out that Dallas' Pegasus must be allowed to fly once again. As we ended the century that saw our city rise to greatness, it seemed fitting that we begin the new era with the symbol of our city intact. This year-long project, supported by local charities, foundations, and private donations, required that an exact duplicate be made and outlined with red neon glass, and a totally modernized ball-bearing turntable be installed to support it and to allow the horse to revolve slowly, to look out to all parts of Dallas. On New Years Eve 1999, in front of a crowd of over forty thousand excited onlookers at the corner of Main and Akard, the mayor of Dallas turned the switch. All heads looked up to see Pegasus return to life, glowing bright red in the night sky, and then to begin turning slowly and gracefully, making its clockwise revolutions, assuring all who were present that for generations to come Pegasus will retain the significance of what this city is and dreams to be.

STREAMING DOWN A HILLSIDE AT PIONEER PLAZA
NEAR THE DALLAS CONVENTION CENTER IN DOWN-
TOWN. (RIGHT) PEGASUS FLIES ATOP THE MAGNOLIA
BUILDING WHILE AN IMPENDING RAIN STORM DRAMATI-
CALLY FRAMES THE DOWNTOWN AREA.

THE BUSY CITY OF DALLAS GLOWS ON THE HORIZON AT DUSK, AS SEEN FROM THE FRENCH-INSPIRED CRESCENT COURT HOTEL.

IN 1934, IN HONOR OF THE ANNUAL MEETING OF THE AMERICAN PETROLEUM INSTITUTE IN DALLAS, THE MAGNOLIA PETROLEUM COMPANY ERECTED A GIANT, REVOLVING VERSION OF THE COMPANY TRADEMARK ATOP ITS HEADQUARTERS BUILDING ON COMMERCE STREET. THE BRIGHTLY LIT RED HORSE BECAME A BEACON VISIBLE FOR MILES, A LANDMARK FOR RESIDENTS AND VISITORS ALIKE. RESTORED IN 1999, PEGASUS AGAIN REVOLVES AGAINST THE SKY.

THE NAME OF REUNION TOWER RECALLS THE UTOPIAN FRENCH SOCIALIST COMMUNITY THAT WAS SETTLED THREE MILES WEST IN 1855.
ITS REVOLVING GEODESIC DOME WITH ITS NIGHTLY LIGHT SHOW IS AN EXPRESSION OF THE WONDERS OF MODERN TECHNOLOGY.

(OPPOSITE) BUILT IN 1903 BY RANCHER AND BANKER J. B. WILSON AND PATTERNED AFTER PARIS'S GRAND OPERA HOUSE, THE WILSON BUILDING WAS CONSIDERED THE PREMIER COMMERCIAL STRUCTURE WEST OF THE MISSISSIPPI. THE ELEGANT BUILDING AT MAIN, ERVAY, AND ELM STREETS HAS RECENTLY BEEN TRANSFORMED INTO LUXURY LOFT APARTMENTS. (ABOVE) RENOWNED BRITISH SCULPTOR HENRY MOORE CREATED THIS MONUMENTAL SCULPTURE FOR CITY HALL PLAZA IN 1978. CALLED "THE DALLAS PIECE", IT IS 16 FEET HIGH, 24 FEET WIDE, AND WEIGHS 27,000 POUNDS.

(ABOVE) CREATED IN THE 1930S AS A CEREMONIAL ENTRY INTO
DALLAS, THE TRIPLE UNDERPASS AND DEALEY PLAZA GAINED A
TRAGIC PLACE IN HISTORY WHEN PRESIDENT JOHN F. KENNEDY
WAS ASSASSINATED THERE WHILE RIDING IN A MOTORCADE
THROUGH DOWNTOWN DALLAS ON NOVEMBER 22, 1963. (LEFT) IN
1970, PHILIP JOHNSON DESIGNED A SIMPLE CENOTAPH (TOMB
WITHOUT A BODY) FOR AN OTHERWISE FEATURELESS PLAZA NEXT
TO "OLD RED" TO EXPRESS THE CITY'S LINGERING ANGUISH IN
THE YEARS FOLLOWING THE 1963 ASSASSINATION OF PRESIDENT

JOHN F. KENNEDY. IN THE DISTANCE, A PRIMITIVE LOG CABIN
SIMILAR TO THAT OCCUPIED BY JOHN NEELY BRYAN, THE
FOUNDER OF DALLAS, SERVES AS A REMINDER OF THE CITY'S
HUMBLE ORIGINS. (RIGHT) THE PLAZA IN FRONT OF DALLAS
CITY HALL ENCOMPASSES TWO CITY BLOCKS AND INCLUDES A
REFLECTING POOL WITH A DIAMETER OF 180 FEET, A VARIABLE-
HEIGHT FOUNTAIN, PARK BENCHES, AND THREE DISTINCTIVE
84-FOOT-HIGH FLAGPOLES. THE PLAZA IS LANDSCAPED WITH
LIVE OAKS AND RED OAKS—TREES NATIVE TO TEXAS.

(OPPOSITE) THIS ONE VIEW CAPTURES THREE DIFFERENT ERAS IN DALLAS HISTORY—
THE PIONEER PERIOD (SYMBOLIZED BY THE SIMPLE LOG CABIN IN THE FOREGROUND), THE
LATE 19TH CENTURY WHEN DALLAS BECAME THE COMMERCIAL CENTER FOR NORTH
TEXAS (SYMBOLIZED BY THE "OLD RED" COURTHOUSE), AND THE MODERN ERA (REPRE-
SENTED BY REUNION TOWER). (ABOVE) THE ELABORATE IRONWORK OF THE INTERIOR
STAIRCASES INSIDE THE "OLD RED" COURTHOUSE TESTIFIES TO THE CAREFUL CRAFTS-
MANSHIP THAT WENT INTO DALLAS COUNTY'S MOST IMPORTANT PUBLIC BUILDING.
EQUAL CARE IS BEING DEVOTED TO RESTORING THE STRUCTURE AND CREATING A
MUSEUM OF DALLAS COUNTY HISTORY AND CULTURE WITHIN, PLANNED TO OPEN IN 2006.

(ABOVE LEFT) BEER BARON ADOLPHUS BUSCH SPARED NO EXPENSE IN CONSTRUCTING HIS GRAND HOTEL ON COMMERCE STREET IN 1912. CARVINGS REPRESENTING DAY AND NIGHT CROWN THE BAROQUE PEDIMENT OVER THE ENTRY. (ABOVE RIGHT) THE FRENCH ROOM IN THE ADOLPHUS HOTEL HAS CONSISTENTLY RANKED AS ONE OF THE FINEST RESTAURANTS IN DALLAS, OFFERING CONTINENTAL CUISINE IN A EUROPEAN, BAROQUE SETTING. (OPPOSITE LEFT) PHILIP JOHNSON DESIGNED THE CRESCENT, JUST NORTH OF DOWNTOWN, FOR CAROLYN

ROSE HUNT IN THE MID-1980S. IN ADDITION TO OFFICES, RESTAURANTS, AND A HOTEL, IT OFFERS SOME OF THE FINEST UPSCALE FASHION AND ART RETAILERS IN THE CITY. (ABOVE RIGHT) MANSION ON TURTLE CREEK HOTEL DINING. HOUSED WITHIN THE 10,000-SQ.-FT. SHEPPARD KING MANSION, AN AWARD-WINNING RESTAURANT INCLUDES SMALL, INTIMATE PRIVATE DINING AREAS, AS WELL AS A MAIN DINING ROOM WITH AN ADJACENT ENCLOSED VERANDA. PATRONS ENJOY CHEF DEAN FEARING'S SIGNATURE SOUTHWESTERN CUISINE.

The Arts

THE STATE OF THE ARTS   Dolores Barzune

The state of the arts in Dallas is at unprecedented level of achievement. Through enlightened leadership of former city government, we bask in the glow of wonderful community support. With the building of our two latest architectural marvels, the Latino Cultural Center by Richardo Legorreta and the Nasher Sculpture Garden by Renzo Piano, we are on the cusp of a building explosion in the arts district. Joining the ranks of I. M. Pei's Meyerson Symphony Center and Edward Larrabee Barnes's Dallas Museum of Art will be the Winspear Opera Hall by Sir Norman Foster, the Wyly Theatre by Rem Koolhaus, and the renovation and expansion of historical landmark Booker T. Washington High School for the Performing and Visual Arts by Brad Cloepfil. In a few short years we will go a long way to fulfill the Arts District dream of a comprehensive arts center with outstanding architecture.

Along with all these architectural landmarks the arts community continues to expand and grow. The small emerging and medium-size groups are continuing to extend services as they strengthen their art form, while the major arts institutions continue to exert their influences and share their talents with the rest of the community. Each discipline is continuing to look to the future with vision, fiscal responsibility, and collaborative spirit.

At the same time, we are throwing wide the doors and windows to the minds of Dallas children by providing them with the keys to succeed. The freedom to create, the freedom to feel, and the freedom to learn and experience the unfamiliar—that's what an arts education can do for children. Humanity needs a reason to live, and the arts give you a sense of connection to life. Just the artistic process itself is one in which you have to focus and concentrate on many thoughtful and energizing levels.

The arts in Dallas endeavor to feed the heart and soul of our city with beauty and wonder as we go about our business of improving all art forms. John F. Kennedy said, "The life of the arts, far from being an interruption, a distraction, in the life of a nation, is close to the center of a nation's purpose—and is a test of the quality of a nation's civilization."

In Dallas we are blessed because our arts community understands the important role we play in the vitality of our city. We also serve as an economic engine for the city's plans to capture the state's tourist business and make Dallas a great art center destination. Dallas will soon be the recognizable arts mecca for Texas.

(PRECEDING SPREAD) DESIGNED BY I. M. PEI, THE MORTON MEYERSON SYMPHONY CENTER OPENED IN 1989 AS A KEY COMPONENT OF THE DALLAS ARTS DISTRICT. THE NEW HOME OF THE DALLAS SYMPHONY ORCHESTRA IMMEDIATELY DREW RAVE REVIEWS FOR ITS OUTSTANDING ACOUSTICS. (ABOVE) ARCHITECT RICARDO LEGORRETA COMBINED THE WARM EARTH TONES OF LATIN AMERICA WITH THE COOLNESS OF WATER IN HIS NEW LATINO CULTURAL CENTER.

ART AND PHILANTHROPY Raymond D. Nasher

The opening of the Nasher Sculpture Center in the Dallas Arts District in the fall of 2003, was the culmination of a half century of art collecting by me and, until her sad death in 1988, my late wife Patsy. We started in 1950 with pre-Columbian art. At that time, we were not thinking about building a major collection, but were acting solely from the joy of surrounding ourselves with beautiful objects created by the mind and hands of an ancient civilization. Art had always been important to us; our families exposed us to it from early ages, and Patsy enhanced her knowledge and stoked her enthusiasm for art through her studies at Smith College. But our interest was entirely personal—selfish, if you like—since our only goal was to enhance our home environment for our personal pleasure and the intellectual stimulation of ourselves and our children.

From that modest beginning, we extended our interest to modern sculpture and developed a passion for collecting that has lasted for decades and resulted in a collection that now numbers more than three hundred pieces. It starts with Rodin and Gauguin, proceeds through works by Matisse, Picasso, Giacommeti, and other modernists, and extends to contemporary artists, such as Magdalena Abakanowicz, Richard Serra, Mark di Suvero and Joel Shapiro.

By the mid-1980s, Patsy and I had been persuaded by knowledgeable people in the art world that we had assembled an important and unique survey of the history of modern sculpture that should be exposed to the public. Consequently, the collection was exhibited in major museums in Dallas, Washington, D.C., Madrid, Florence, and Tel Aviv in 1988-89. In 1986-87, it traveled to the San Francisco Museum of Art and the New York Guggenheim.

Although personally pleased and gratified that, after its initial tour, the collection had become internationally admired, my family and I hadn't given much thought to what should happen to it after Patsy and I were both gone, except to decide that we wanted to turn our private passion into a public treasure. We rejected the perfectly admirable philanthropic route of bequeathing individual pieces, or groups of pieces, to various museums throughout the country, since this would destroy the coherence of the collection. Instead, we adopted two goals: first, to keep the works together, and second, to make them easily accessible to the public. One way to fulfill both aims would have been to graft the collection as a whole

onto an existing museum—and discussions were held along these lines with several prominent institutions. In the end, however, we decided that the ultimate gift would be for my family's Nasher Foundation to fully finance the construction of a sculpture center designed to house and exhibit our collection. We decided to do this in our home city of Dallas, where Patsy and our daughters had been born, and where I had had my own good fortune in business.

The Nasher Sculpture Center, designed by prize-winning architect Renzo Piano and noted landscape architect Peter Walker, has created the only sculpture garden anywhere in a truly urban setting. We are proud of this, and value equally the fact that we have joined a group of small museums—including the Menil in Houston, the Kimbell in Fort Worth, the Pulitzer in St. Louis and the Neue in New York—that exhibit private collections in facilities paid for entirely by the collectors themselves. My family and I take pride in being part of this distinguished company.

SITUATED IN DOWNTOWN DALLAS AT THE BASE OF THE CITY'S SKYLINE, THE NASHER SCULPTURE CENTER REPRESENTS RAY NASHER'S VISION TO CREATE AN OUTDOOR "ROOFLESS" MUSEUM THAT WILL SERVE AS A PEACEFUL RETREAT FOR REFLECTION ON ART AND NATURE AND A PUBLIC HOME FOR HIS COLLECTION OF 20TH-CENTURY SCULPTURE.

TRACING ITS ORIGINS TO A PUBLIC ART GALLERY IN THE OLD 1901 CARNEGIE LIBRARY, THE DALLAS MUSEUM OF ART MOVED INTO ITS CURRENT FACILITY IN THE ARTS DISTRICT IN 1984. DESIGNED BY EDWARD LARRABEE BARNES, THE FACILITY WELCOMES VISITORS FROM ITS ENTRY PLAZA INTO A SOARING BARREL VAULT WITH FOUR LEVELS OF GALLERIES BEYOND.

THE DALLAS THEATER CENTER, THE CITY'S OLDEST PROFESSIONAL THEATER COMPANY, OCCUPIES THE ONLY THEATER DESIGNED BY FRANK LLOYD WRIGHT. CONSTRUCTED IN 1959 ON THE BANKS OF TURTLE CREEK, THE BUILDING IS AN EXERCISE IN CURVES AND ANGLES—NONE OF THEM RIGHT ANGLES.

THIS SCULPTURE OF BUDDHA IS AMONG THE HIGHLIGHTS OF
THE TRAMMELL AND MARGARET CROW COLLECTION OF ASIAN ART, WHICH CONTAINS MORE THAN 600 PAINTINGS,
OBJECTS OF METAL AND STONE, AND LARGE ARCHITECTURAL PIECES FROM CHINA, JAPAN, AND THE FAR EAST.

THIS EXHIBIT SPACE AT THE DALLAS MUSEUM OF ART IS FILLED WITH ASIAN ARTIFACTS.

(OPPOSITE) THE FAIR PARK MUSIC HALL WAS BUILT IN 1925 AND DESIGNED BY LANG & WITCHELL. THE DESIGN INCORPORATES SPANISH COLO-NIAL REVIVAL WITH DOMINATING SQUARE TOWERS. HOME TO THE DALLAS SUMMER MUSICALS, THE DALLAS OPERA AND THE TEXAS BALLET THEATRE, THE MUSIC HALL ATTRACTS LARGE CROWDS SEEKING TOP-LEVEL ENTERTAINMENT. (ABOVE) MEMBERS OF A DANCE TROUPE PREPARE TO PERFORM AT THE ASIAN FESTIVAL IN ANNETTE STRAUSS ARTISTS SQUARE.

SMU'S MEADOWS MUSEUM COMMISSIONED SPANISH ARTIST SANTIAGO CALATRAVA TO CREATE THIS PERPETUALLY-MOVING SCULPTURE FOR THE STREET-LEVEL PLAZA IN FRONT OF THE MUSEUM. "THE WAVE" CONSISTS OF 129 ROCKING BRONZE BARS RUNNING ITS LENGTH, WHICH MOVE SEQUENTIALLY TO CREATE A FOUR-CYCLE WAVE MOTION IN THE SPACE ABOVE THE REFLECTING POOL. (OPPOSITE) ARISTIDE MALLIOL'S *THREE GRACES* OCCUPY A PROMINENT PLACE IN THE MEADOWS MUSEUM OF ART, WHICH HOUSES ONE OF THE LARGEST AND MOST COMPRE-HENSIVE COLLECTIONS OF SPANISH ART OUTSIDE SPAIN.

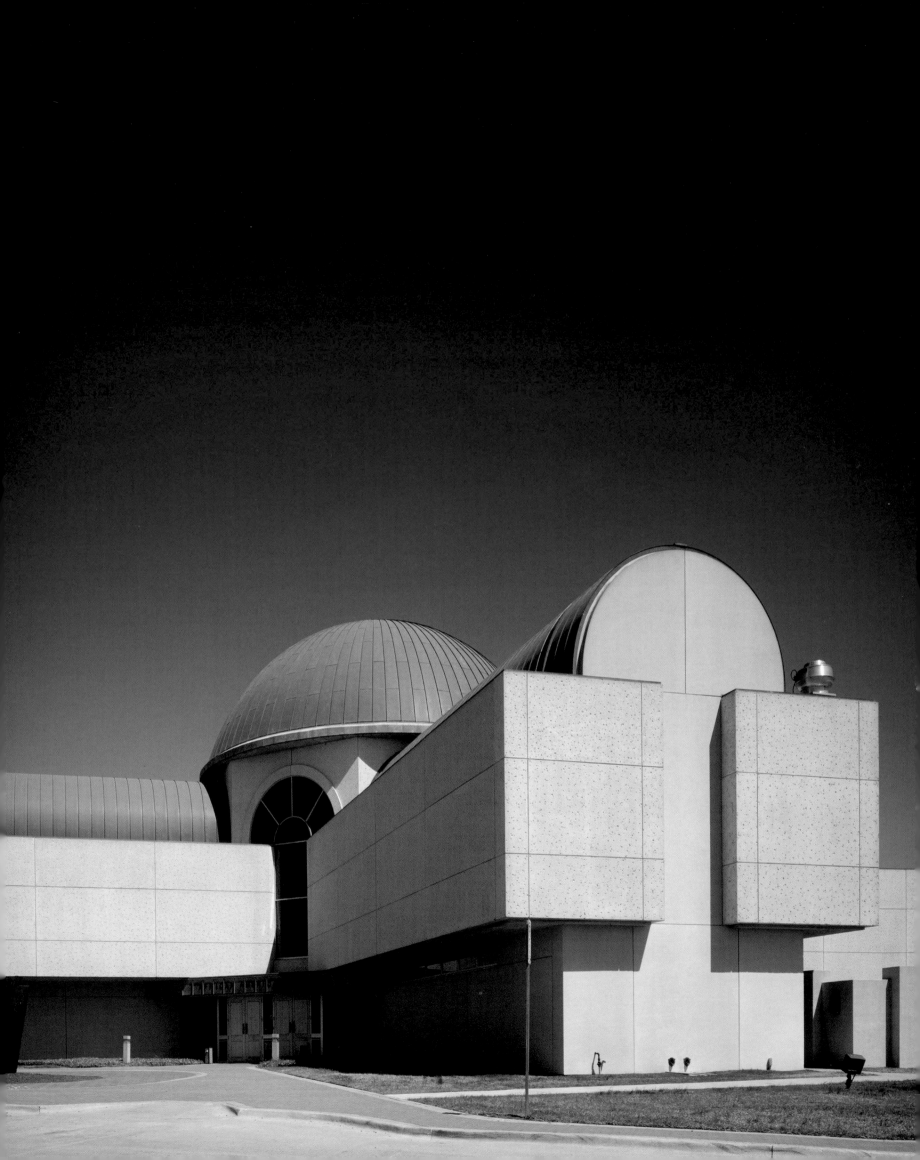

(OPPOSITE) ARTHUR J. ROGERS DESIGNED THE AFRICAN AMERICAN MUSEUM IN THE SHAPE OF A TRADITIONAL AFRICAN CROSS, ITS DOMED WINGS HOUSING GALLERIES DEVOTED TO ART, CULTURE, AND HISTORY. OPENED IN 1993, THE MUSEUM STANDS NEAR THE SITE OF THE NEGRO HALL OF FAME, BUILT WITH FEDERAL FUNDS FOR THE TEXAS CENTENNIAL EXPOSITION IN 1936 OVER LOCAL OPPOSITION, AND DEMOLISHED THE FOLLOWING YEAR. (THIS PAGE TOP) YOUNG MUSICIANS REHEARSE BEFORE A PERFORMANCE AT ANNETTE STRAUSS ARTISTS SQUARE OUTSIDE THE MEYERSON SYMPHONY CENTER. (THIS PAGE CENTER) AN EXHIBIT AT THE AFRICAN AMERICAN MUSEUM INCLUDES A BOTTLE TREE— A COLLECTION OF BOTTLES REPRESENTING LOST SPIRITS AND SHOWING THE SACREDNESS OF RITUAL. NOTES AND TWIGS ARE OFTEN PUT INSIDE THE BOTTLES. (THIS PAGE BOTTOM) ARTISTS SHOW THEIR UNIQUE CREATIONS AT VARIOUS ARTS AND CRAFT FAIRS IN THE CITY. THIS ARTIST SPORTS APPROPRIATE ATTIRE TO ATTRACT ONLOOKERS AND POTENTIAL PATRONS.

THE LATINO CULTURAL CENTER, DESIGNED BY ARCHITECT RICARDO LEGORRETA, IS THE REALIZATION OF A VISION FOSTERED BY DALLAS CITIZENS FOR A CITY FACILITY THAT WOULD ARTISTICALLY, RESPECTFULLY, AND AUTHENTICALLY REFLECT AND REPRESENT THE LATINO COMMUNITY'S RICH HISTORICAL CULTURE. THE CENTER OFFERS OPPORTUNITIES FOR EDUCATION AND EXPERIENCES IN QUALITY MUSIC, THEATRE, DANCE, VISUAL, LITERARY, MEDIA, AND TRADITIONAL ARTS. (OPPOSITE TOP AND BOTTOM) YOUNG DANCERS PERFORM AT ONE OF SEVERAL ARTS FESTIVALS DOWNTOWN.

THE 1,570-SEAT MAJESTIC THEATER WAS ONCE ONE OF DOZENS OF
VAUDEVILLE AND MOVIE PALACES LINING ELM STREET. TODAY IT IS THE
SOLE REMINDER OF AN ERA WHEN AREA RESIDENTS FLOCKED TO DOWN-
TOWN DALLAS FOR ENTERTAINMENT. CONSTRUCTED IN 1921, THE THEATER
WAS DONATED TO THE CITY IN 1979 AND HAS BEEN CAREFULLY RESTORED
FOR USE BY TOURING DANCE, THEATER, AND MUSICAL COMPANIES.

Parks and Plazas

(PRECEEDING SPREAD) *THE MUSTANGS OF LAS COLINAS*, IN WILLIAMS SQUARE PLAZA, TOOK SCULPTOR ROBERT GLEN SEVEN YEARS TO COMPLETE. THE NINE BRONZE, LARGER-THAN-LIFE HORSES GALLOPING THROUGH A CASCADING STREAM COMPRISE THE LARGEST EQUESTRIAN SCULPTURE IN THE WORLD. (ABOVE AND OPPOSITE) FOUNTAIN PLACE HAS BEEN CALLED THE MOST EXTRAORDINARY OF I. M. PEI'S DALLAS BUILDINGS, A 60-STORY MINIMALIST SCULPTURE SHEATHED IN SHIMMERING GREEN GLASS, THE SIX-ACRE PLAZA AND SUBLIME WATER GARDEN AT ITS BASE SOFTEN THE HARD-EDGED GEOMETRY OF THE STRUCTURE AND CREATE ONE OF THE MOST ENTRANCING URBAN SPACES IN DALLAS.

THANKSGIVING, DESIGNED BY PHILIP JOHNSON, THANKS-GIVING SQUARE AND ITS UNIQUE INTERFAITH CHAPEL IN
THE MIDDLE OF DOWNTOWN DALLAS PROVIDE A HAVEN FOR REST AND MEDITATION TO DOWNTOWN WORKERS AND VISITORS ALIKE.

THE GLORY WINDOW, WHICH FORMS THE 60-FOOT-HIGH CEILING OF THE CHAPEL OF THANKSGIVING AT THANKS-GIVING SQUARE, IS ONE OF THE LARGEST HORIZONTALLY MOUNTED, STAINED-GLASS PIECES IN THE WORLD. DESIGNED BY FRENCH ARTIST GABRIEL LOIRE, THE WINDOW SYMBOLIZES THE BLESSING OF THE DIVINE DESCENDING TO EARTH AS WELL AS THE ASCENT OF HUMAN PRAISE AND GRATITUDE TO GOD.

(OPPOSITE) THIS QUEEN ANNE-STYLE HOUSE, COMPLETE WITH TURRET AND GINGERBREAD TRIM, WAS BUILT BY A HARDWARE MERCHANT IN THE TOWN OF PLANO AS A WEDDING PRESENT FOR HIS WIFE IN 1900. TODAY IT HAS BEEN RESTORED AT OLD CITY PARK, THE HISTORICAL VILLAGE OF DALLAS. (ABOVE) EAST TEXAS OIL MILLIONAIRE H. L. HUNT PURCHASED THIS REPLICA OF MOUNT VERNON IN THE LATE 1930S WHEN HE MOVED HIS FAMILY TO DALLAS. LOCATED ON THE WEST SHORE OF WHITE ROCK LAKE, THE HOUSE HAS RECENTLY BEEN RESTORED AND ENLARGED BY NEW OWNERS.

PRESIDENT FRANKLIN D. ROOSEVELT UNVEILED THIS STATUE OF GENERAL ROBERT E. LEE AND AN AIDE DURING A VISIT TO THE TEXAS CENTENNIAL EXPOSITION IN JUNE, 1936. LOCATED ABOVE TURTLE CREEK, THE PARK, ORIGINALLY KNOWN AS OAK LAWN, WAS RENAMED LEE PARK AT THAT TIME. (OPPOSITE) WHEN HALL OFFICE PARK OPENED, IT BECAME ONE OF THE FIRST LOCAL DEVELOPMENTS TO INTEGRATE SCULPTURE INTO A LONG-RANGE MASTER PLAN. CHOSEN AS DEMONSTRATIONS OF THE EXCELLENCE AND DIVERSITY OF BOTH MATERIALS AND STYLES FROM AROUND THE STATE, THE THREE DOZEN WORKS FEATURED IN THE TEXAS SCULPTURE GARDEN WERE PRODUCED BY ARTISTS LIVING IN LARGE CITIES SUCH AS DALLAS, HOUSTON, AND SAN ANTONIO, AS WELL AS RURAL TOWNS SUCH AS SANGER, BOLIVAR, AND OVILLA. *SPIRE* IS ONE OF EIGHT INSTALLATIONS BY J. BROUGH MILLER OF ARGYLE, TEXAS.

(OPPOSITE) A GIGANTIC GIRAFFE LOOMING HIGH OVER R. L. THORNTON FREEWAY BECKONS VISITORS TO THE DALLAS ZOO, LOCATED IN MARSALIS PARK IN OAK CLIFF. THE ZOO FEATURES A VARIETY OF HABITATS FOR ITS MORE THAN 1,500 ANIMALS. (THIS PAGE TOP LEFT) A WOULD-BE RODEO PERFORMER PLAYS ON ONE OF THE BRONZE CATTLE AT PIONEER PLAZA. (THIS PAGE BOTTOM LEFT) THE PETTING ZOO HOSTS AN ANNUAL OAK LAWN FESTIVAL. (THIS PAGE ABOVE RIGHT) A ZOO ATTENDANT HOLDS A MAGNIFICENT HYACINTH MACAW.

WATER MISTERS PROVIDE NOT ONLY THE IDEAL HABITAT FOR FERNS AT THE DALLAS ARBORETUM, BUT AN OTHERWORLDLY EXPERIENCE FOR VISITORS.

(ABOVE LEFT) WINDING ITS WAY FROM THE PARK CITIES THROUGH OAK LAWN AND EVENTUALLY TO THE TRINITY RIVER, TURTLE CREEK SERVES BOTH NATURE LOVERS AND SPORTS ENTHUSIASTS WITH ITS WATERFOWL, LANDSCAPED BANKS, JOGGING AND BIKING TRAILS, AND SEVERAL PARKS. (ABOVE RIGHT) ORIGINALLY DEVELOPED AS AN AMUSEMENT PARK IN THE EARLY 20TH CENTURY, LAKE CLIFF PARK, LOCATED JUST ACROSS THE TRINITY RIVER FROM DOWNTOWN DALLAS, IS NOW THE CENTER OF AN OAK CLIFF HISTORIC DISTRICT, SURROUNDED BY STATELY OLDER

HOMES, NEW APARTMENTS, AND UNIQUE SHOPS AND RESTAURANTS. (ABOVE LEFT) WHITE ROCK LAKE SPILLWAY. BIRDWATCHERS FIND THE SPILLWAY AT WHITE ROCK LAKE AND THE HEAVILY WOODED SITE NEARBY IDEAL FOR SPOTTING COLORFUL SPECIES. (ABOVE RIGHT) ALTHOUGH IGNORED BY MOST DALLASITES, THE TRINITY RIVER STILL FLOWS THROUGH THE HEART OF THE CITY, OFTEN HIDDEN FROM VIEW BY ONE OF THE LARGEST URBAN FORESTS IN THE NATION.

(OPPOSITE TOP) RAINDROPS HANG ON GRASSES AND RED FLOWERS AT THE DALLAS ARBORETUM. (OPPOSITE BOTTOM) THE TRINITY RIVER WET-
LANDS ABOUND WITH WILDLIFE, SUCH AS THESE CRANES. (ABOVE) A TRANQUIL WOODLAND STREAM WELCOMES VISITORS TO THE FERN DELL
AT THE DALLAS ARBORETUM. COMPRISING BOTH THE HISTORIC DEGOLYER AND CAMP ESTATES ALONG THE EASTERN SHORE OF WHITE ROCK
LAKE, THE ARBORETUM SHOWCASES A WIDE VARIETY OF FLOWERS, TREES, AND SHRUBBERY IN BOTH FORMAL AND INFORMAL GARDENS.

(ABOVE) NAMED FOR THE LONG-TIME GARDENER WHO PRUNED THIS
WINDOW THROUGH THE FOLIAGE, "JOE'S HOLE" FRAMES A VIEW OF
WHITE ROCK LAKE FROM ONE OF THE GARDENS AT THE DALLAS
ARBORETUM. (FAR LEFT) PINK WITH SEEDS (RIGHT) PASSION FLOWER.
NAMED FOR THE PASSION OF CHRIST, THIS INTRICATE INDIGENOUS
FLOWER-VINE INHABITS THE FIELDS AND GARDENS OF TEXAS. THE
FRUIT IS EDIBLE AND DELICIOUS.

FAST-GROWING MIMOSA TREES HAVE HOT CHERRY-PINK BLOSSOMS, AND WILL CREATE AN EXCEPTIONAL UMBRELLA OF
FERN-LIKE FOLIAGE. THESE TREES CAN TOLERATE EXTREME TEXAS HEAT AND OCCASIONAL DROUGHT.

THE COMMON THISTLE, A PLANT IN THE ASTER FAMILY, HAS LARGE, COARSE STEMS WITH SPINY LEAVES.
A SECTION OF THE THISTLE BUD MAKES AN INTRIGUING DESIGN FROM NATURE.

(OPPOSITE) BLUEBONNETS AND INDIAN PAINTBRUSH. A PALETTE OF RED, YELLOW AND BLUE TEXAS WILDFLOWERS GRACE THE LOCAL DALLAS LANDSCAPE. (ABOVE LEFT) BLUEBONNETS BEGIN BLOOMING IN THE EARLY SPRING. ALL SIX SPECIES OF BLUEBONNET THAT GROW IN THE STATE HAVE BEEN DESIGNATED THE STATE FLOWER BY THE TEXAS LEGISLATURE. (ABOVE RIGHT) CONE FLOWERS, MORE COMMONLY SEEN AS PURPLE CONE FLOWERS, ARE NATIVE TO NORTH AMERICA, GROWING GENERALLY IN DRY AREAS LIKE GRASSLANDS AND STONY OUT-CROPPINGS AND IN OPEN, FORESTED AREAS. (FOLLOWING SPREAD) ALTHOUGH MOST OF DALLAS COUNTY IS NOW URBAN, WITH 26 INCORPORATED COMMUNITIES, PARCELS OF RURAL ACREAGE REMAIN, WHERE CATTLE AND WILDFLOWERS PEACEFULLY COEXIST.

Fair Park and
The State Fair of Texas

Fair Park and The State Fair of Texas Nancy Wiley

It is impossible to separate the histories of Fair Park and the State Fair of Texas. Without the property and popularity of the State Fair, which traces its origins in that location to 1886, there would never have been a Fair Park. And without Fair Park's magnificent architecture, multiple museums, Music Hall, and Cotton Bowl, the State Fair of Texas would not have reached its preeminent status among annual expositions in the United States.

Dallas voters supported the purchase of the fairgrounds from the privately incorporated State Fair Association in 1904, and the 117 acres of race track, gardens, exhibit buildings, and livestock barns became the second park in the city system. A contract stipulated that the organizers of the State Fair of Texas would continue to present the grand event each fall on what was now city-owned property. The same agreement, updated and revised over the years, still defines the park's operation.

Fair Park and the State Fair of Texas prospered together through the early years of the twentieth century. In 1934, banker R. L. Thornton put together a proposal for Dallas and Fair Park to host the 1936 Texas Centennial Exposition. The bid, endorsed by the State Fair Board, had a total value of $9.5 million, nearly double that of the nearest competitor, and Dallas was selected as the site for the central celebration. A new Fair Park was built by an army of more than eight thousand laborers in less than a year at an estimated cost of $25 million. The physical plant consisted of more than fifty structures, waterways, massive pylons, terraces, statues, and murals expressed in an innovative architectural styling variously described as Art Deco, Texas Colonial, Southwestern Classical, or simply Texanic. Like most large-scale fairs, the six-month Texas Centennial Exposition did not make money. Its success would be measured by the attention it focused on the southwest, by the impact it had in revitalizing the local economy, by the new products and processes—particularly air conditioning of public spaces—that it introduced into everyday life and by the distinctive blend of art, architecture, and landscaping which was its legacy. Today Fair Park boasts the largest collection of exposition buildings still intact from the golden era of world fairs. The 277-acre park was designated a National Historic Landmark in 1985. It is home to nine museums, three performance venues, a 72,000-seat stadium and numerous multi-purpose facilities. In recent years, public and private funds have been used to repaint the buildings and restore the murals, frescoes, fixtures, and lighting to echo the majesty of the Centennial. The banners, flags, and twinkling lights added each fall during the annual run of the great State Fair show the park to its best advantage.

The State Fair of Texas is recognized as the nation's largest and most successful state fair. It is distinguished by an entertainment lineup that includes college football games, a wall-to-wall new car show, major cultural exhibits, wildlife conservation shows, the national touring company production of a Broadway musical, and free outdoor concerts by big name stars, as well as the time-honored fare of livestock sales, cooking contests, and midway rides.

The Fair provides an opportunity for Dallas to let its hair down and host a rollicking party for the entire state. For twenty-four days in late September and October, "Big Tex", the inimitable fifty-two-foot tall, talking-cowboy icon, welcomes fairgoers to his neon playground, and the Fletcher family sells more than 550,000 corny dogs to people who have waited eleven long months for another chance to savor this invented-in-Texas delicacy.

The State Fair is a melting pot and a meeting place for more than three million visitors each year. It is an amalgam of sunshine, crowds, noise, and tantalizing aromas. Above all, the Fair is fun, and it serves to shine a spotlight on the wondrous park that bears its name.

(PRECEDING SPREAD) THE ESPLANADE, WITH REFLECTING POOLS FLANKED BY EXHIBITION BUILDINGS AND CROWNED BY THE HALL OF STATE, WAS THE CENTERPIECE OF ARCHITECT GEORGE DAHL'S DESIGN FOR THE TEXAS CENTENNIAL EXPOSITION IN 1936. (OPPOSITE) FUN-LOVERS CAN RENT BOATS SHAPED AS SWANS AND DUCKS AT THE LAGOON AT FAIR PARK. (ABOVE) FEW VISITORS GET TO SEE THIS SPECTACULAR VIEW OF THE CITY FROM THE ROOF OF THE HALL OF STATE. THE VIEW STRETCHES DOWN THE ESPLANADE WITH THE SKYLINE OF DOWNTOWN DALLAS IN THE DISTANCE.

(OPPOSITE) RAOUL JOSSET CREATED THIS GRACEFUL SCULPTURE OF A WOMAN, ENTITLED *SPIRIT OF THE CENTENNIAL*, IN 1936 FOR THE TEXAS CENTENNIAL EXPOSITION. THE SCULPTURE AND THE TEXAS-THEMED MURAL BEHIND IT, BY CARLO CIAMPAGLIA, WERE RECENTLY RESTORED IN HONOR OF CALVERT COLLINS, THE FIRST WOMAN TO SERVE ON THE DALLAS CITY COUNCIL. (ABOVE) SIX ENORMOUS STATUES LINE THE ESPLANADE, EACH REPRESENTING ONE OF THE NATIONS WHOSE FLAG HAS FLOWN OVER TEXAS—SPAIN, FRANCE, MEXICO, THE REPUBLIC OF TEXAS, THE CONFEDERACY, AND THE UNITED STATES.

BUILT BY THE STATE OF TEXAS FOR THE 1936 CENTENNIAL EXPOSITION, THE HALL OF STATE HAS HOSTED EVENTS HONORING
PRESIDENTS, ROYALTY, HEADS OF STATE, AND OTHER DIGNITARIES FOR OVER SIXTY YEARS.

THE NEWLY RESTORED *SPIRIT OF THE CENTENNIAL* PROVIDES THE FOCAL POINT FOR
THE ENTRANCE TO THE WOMEN'S MUSEUM: AN INSTITUTE FOR THE FUTURE.

(TOP) ARTIST JAMES BUCHANAN (BUCK) WINN CARVED THIS INTRICATE CONCRETE FRIEZE AT THE BASE OF THE TOWERING PYLON MARKING THE CEREMONIAL ENTRANCE TO FAIR PARK. IT DEPICTS A GROUP OF SETTLERS CROSSING THE PLAINS ON THEIR WAY TO TEXAS. (ABOVE) COWBOYS PERFORMING AT THE DALLAS BLACK COWBOY RODEO RECALL THE STATE'S WESTERN HERITAGE.

LOCAL POLICE AND FIRE DEPARTMENTS PROVIDE THEIR CADETS WITH RIGOROUS TRAINING,
THE RESULT OF WHICH CAN BE SEEN IN DALLAS' FINEST, WHO PATROL THE CITY ON THEIR VARIOUS MOUNTS.

(OPPOSITE) DINOSAUR BONES UNEARTHED IN NORTH TEXAS ARE AMONG THE MOST POPULAR ATTRACTIONS AT THE DALLAS MUSEUM OF NATURAL HISTORY IN FAIR PARK. (TOP LEFT) *JUMBO*, A MAMMOTH SCULPTED BY TOM TISCHLER, STANDS OUTSIDE THE DALLAS MUSEUM OF NATURAL HISTORY. IT WAS MODELED AFTER A FOSSIL EXCAVATED IN DALLAS. (TOP RIGHT) AT THE DALLAS MUSEUM OF NATURAL HISTORY, VISITORS CAN STUDY MAMMOTH BONES UNEARTHED IN NORTH TEXAS. (ABOVE) THE FOSSIL REMAINS OF A PREHISTORIC TURTLE AT THE DALLAS MUSEUM OF NATURAL HISTORY ARE A REMINDER THAT THIS REGION ONCE LAY BENEATH THE OCEAN.

MISS CLYDE CHANDLER, A DALLAS SCULPTOR, EXECUTED THIS FOUNTAIN, *GULF CLOUD*, IN 1913 AS A MEMORIAL TO SYDNEY SMITH, LONGTIME EXECUTIVE SECRETARY OF THE STATE FAIR OF TEXAS. THE FOUR FIGURES SYMBOLIZE THE GULF OF MEXICO, THE COASTAL PLAINS, THE TABLE-LANDS, AND THE MOUNTAINS OF WEST TEXAS. (OPPOSITE TOP) ONE OF THE ENDURING LEGACIES OF THE TEXAS CENTENNIAL EXPOSITION WAS DALLAS' FIRST PERMANENT CULTURAL DISTRICT, A COLLECTION OF MUSEUMS AND PERFORMANCE VENUES LOOSELY ORGANIZED AROUND A NATURALISTIC LAGOON. A MAJOR EARTH SCULPTURE WAS ADDED TO THE LAGOON IN 1986. (OPPOSITE BOTTOM) THE RAILROAD ENGINES AND PASSENGER CARS EXHIBITED AT THE AGE OF STEAM MUSEUM AT FAIR PARK RECALL FOR VISITORS THE ERA WHEN THE RAILROADS MADE DALLAS THE TRANSPORTATION CENTER OF NORTH TEXAS.

(TOP) THE ANNUAL HOISTING INTO PLACE OF "BIG TEX" EACH FALL IS EAGERLY DOCUMENTED BY THE LOCAL MEDIA AS A SIGN THAT THE STATE FAIR IS ABOUT TO OPEN. (ABOVE) A FAMILY ENJOYS "CORN ON THE COB" AT THE STATE FAIR. ANOTHER STAPLE OF THE STATE FAIR INCLUDES "CORNY DOGS", A BATTER-FRIED HOT DOG, INVENTED BY NEIL AND CARL FLETCHER, AND INTRODUCED AT THE 1942 TEXAS STATE FAIR. (RIGHT) "BIG TEX" HAS WELCOMED VISITORS TO THE STATE FAIR OF TEXAS EVERY YEAR SINCE 1952. WEARING 70-GALLON BOOTS AND A 75-GALLON HAT, "TEX" TOWERS TO A HEIGHT OF 52 FEET. (FOLLOWING SPREAD, TOP) THE LIGHTS OF THE STATE FAIR OF TEXAS BECKON VISITORS TO THIS, THE LARGEST STATE FAIR IN THE NATION. (FOLLOWING SPREAD, BOTTOM) THE FAMOUS "TEXAS STAR" FERRIS WHEEL PROVIDES A CONSTANT LIGHT SHOW FOR FAIRGOERS.

Sports and Entertainment

(PRECEDING SPREAD) FAIR PARK'S 72,000-SEAT COTTON BOWL, CONSTRUCTED FOR THE 1936 TEXAS CENTENNIAL EXPOSITION, HOSTS THE ANNUAL TEXAS-OKLAHOMA FOOTBALL GAME EACH OCTOBER AS WELL AS OTHER CONTESTS THROUGHOUT THE YEAR. THE DALLAS MUSIC HALL IS VISIBLE IN THE DISTANCE AGAINST THE SKYLINE OF DALLAS. (ABOVE) LOCATED IN ARLINGTON, MIDWAY BETWEEN DALLAS AND FORT WORTH, WHERE THE TEXAS RANGERS PLAY BALL, AMERIQUEST FIELD BOASTS VIEWS TO THE SIX FLAGS OVER TEXAS. (BOTTOM FAR LEFT) TEXAS RANGER. (BOTTOM RIGHT) TEXAS RANGER.

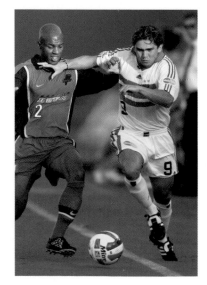

(ABOVE) TEXAS STADIUM. (LEFT) DALLAS COWBOY PLAYERS IN ACTION AT TEXAS STADIUM. (RIGHT) DALLAS BURN SOCCER PLAYERS AT THE COTTON BOWL. (OPPOSITE ABOVE) TEXAS STADIUM IN IRVING IS HOME TO THE DALLAS COWBOYS, "AMERICA'S TEAM", WHICH BECAME THE FIRST TEAM IN NATIONAL FOOTBALL LEAGUE HISTORY TO WIN THREE SUPER BOWLS IN FOUR YEARS. THERE'S A HOLE IN THE ROOF OF THE STADI- UM, LEFT THAT WAY, SOME SAY, SO THAT

GOD COULD WATCH HIS FAVORITE TEAM.
(RIGHT) THE DALLAS COWBOYS
CHEERLEADERS, THE NAME ITSELF BRINGS TO
EACH OF US IMAGES OF AN AMERICAN ICON—
BEAUTIFUL LADIES DECKED OUT IN BLUE AND
WHITE UNIFORMS CHEERING AMERICA'S TEAM
ON TO VICTORY; PRECISION DANCE ROUTINES
THAT REQUIRE A COMBINATION OF STAMINA,
FLEXIBILITY AND TIMING THAT WOULD LEAVE
MOST OF US GASPING. A COMIC PERFORMS
BESIDE THE BEAUTIFUL ONES.

(ABOVE LEFT) AMERICAN AIRLINES CENTER, JUST NORTH OF THE WEST END HISTORIC DISTRICT, OPENED IN JULY 2001, AS HOME TO DALLAS' BASKETBALL AND HOCKEY TEAMS, THE MAVERICKS AND THE STARS. DESIGNED BY RENOWNED ARCHITECT DAVID SCHWARTZ AND DALLAS-BASED HKS, INC., THE CENTER IS A COMBINATION OF TRADITIONAL ARCHITECTURE AND HI-TECH WIZARDRY, WITH RETRACTABLE SEATING THAT BRINGS THE BOWL IN CLOSER TO THE ACTION. (ABOVE RIGHT) MAVERICK PLAYER AND COMPETITOR.

(LEFT) THE ANNUAL BYRON NELSON GOLF TOURNAMENT TEES OFF EACH SPRING AT THE TPC (TOURNAMENT PLAYERS CLUB) COURSE AT LAS COLINAS LOCATED OUTSIDE DALLAS. THE BYRON NELSON RANKS NO. 1 IN CHARITABLE CONTRIBUTIONS ON THE PGA TOUR. (ABOVE) TWO OF THE MOST SCENIC NEIGHBORHOODS IN DALLAS, KESSLER PARK AND STEVENS PARK, WERE DEVELOPED IN THE 1920S AND '30S ALONG HILLY TERRAIN BORDERING CREEKS RUNNING THROUGH NORTH OAK CLIFF. STEVENS PARK GOLF COURSE, ONE OF THE FINEST PUBLIC COURSES IN DALLAS, LINKS THE TWO COMMUNITIES. (FAR RIGHT) TIGER WOODS COMPETES WITH OTHER NATIONALLY KNOWN GOLFERS.

(TOP) WITH ITS WALL-TO-WALL-TO-CEILING COLLECTION OF ROCK'N'ROLL MEMORABILIA, THE HARD ROCK CAFE HAS BECOME A MECCA FOR VIS-
ITING MUSIC FANS AND AN INTIMATE VENUE FOR TOURING ROCK SHOWS. LOCATED IN AN OLD CHURCH BUILDING IN UPTOWN, THE CAFE IS ON
THE MCKINNEY AVENUE STREETCAR LINE, LINKING THE RESTAURANTS AND SHOPS OF MCKINNEY AVENUE WITH DOWNTOWN. (ABOVE) DALLAS
ALLEY IS ONE OF MANY ENTERTAINMENT VENUES THAT HAVE DEVELOPED IN THE HISTORIC WEST END DISTRICT OF DOWNTOWN DALLAS. ONCE
A WAREHOUSE DISTRICT FOR FARM IMPLEMENT DEALERS AND OTHER WHOLESALERS, THE WEST END HAS BECOME ONE OF THE MOST POPULAR
TOURIST DESTINATIONS IN DALLAS. (OPPOSITE) WHIMISICAL ENTRANCE TO SHOPS AT THE WEST END MARKET PLACE. FROM MIDDAY UNTIL LATE
NIGHT, THE SHOPS AT THE WEST END MARKET PLACE ECHO WITH THE SOUNDS OF DALLAS AT PLAY. FOR A DOSE OF ADRENALINE, FOLLOW THE
SOUNDS OF HUNDREDS OF VIDEO GAMES AND AMUSEMENTS THAT LINE THE SPRAWLING LOWER LEVEL OF THE MARKET PLACE.

(OPPOSITE TOP LEFT) ORIGINALLY PART OF A CHAIN OF MOVIE THEATERS OWNED BY HOWARD HUGHES, THE TEXAS THEATER OPENED IN 1931 ON WEST JEFFERSON BLVD. IN OAK CLIFF. IT WAS THE LARGEST SUBURBAN THEATER IN DALLAS, AND THE FIRST TO BOAST AIR CONDITIONING. DALLAS POLICE OFFICERS APPREHENDED LEE HARVEY OSWALD HERE ON NOVEMBER 22, 1963, SHORTLY AFTER THE ASSASSINATION OF PRESIDENT JOHN F. KENNEDY. (OPPOSITE BOTTOM LEFT) LOCATED IN MOCKINGBIRD STATION AND ADJACENT TO A DALLAS AREA RAPID TRANSIT (DART) RAIL STOP, THE ANGELIKA FILM CENTER IS AN EIGHT-SCREEN COMPLEX WITH STADIUM SEATING, DIGITAL SOUND, AND WALL-TO-WALL SCREENS. THE ANGELIKA CAFE, IN THE CINEMA LOBBY, IS AN AMERICAN BISTRO-STYLE RESTAURANT. (OPPOSITE BOTTOM RIGHT) THE INWOOD THEATER ANCHORS ONE OF THE FIRST POST-WORLD WAR II SUBURBAN SHOPPING CENTERS IN DALLAS, ON THE EDGE OF GREENWAY PARKS AND BLUFFVIEW. THE THEATER NOW HOSTS FOREIGN, AVANT GARDE, AND INDE-PENDENT FILMS, AND ITS IN-HOUSE LOUNGE IS A POPULAR NIGHTCLUB. (RIGHT) THE FOREST THEATER ORIGINALLY SERVED THE WHITE, LARGELY JEWISH POPULATION OF SOUTH DALLAS, WHEN FOREST AVENUE WAS LINED WITH KOSHER MARKETS AND FAMILY BUSINESSES. AS THE NEIGHBORHOOD CHANGED, "THE FOREST" BEGAN ATTRACTING AN AFRICAN-AMERICAN AUDIENCE. THE THEATER CLOSED IN 1965, BUT WAS LATER OPERATED AS A CLUB. TODAY SUC-CESSFUL RECORDING ARTIST NORAH JONES, A DALLAS NATIVE, IS SPEARHEADING EFFORTS TO BUY AND RESTORE THE THEATER.

The Business of Dallas

(ABOVE) BAYLOR UNIVERSITY MEDICAL CENTER HAS A RICH HISTO-
RY BEGINNING WITH ITS FOUNDING AS THE TEXAS BAPTIST
MEMORIAL SANITARIUM IN 1903. TODAY THE CENTER PROVIDES
CARE TO THE PATIENTS OF MORE THAN 2,400 PHYSICIANS. (RIGHT)
AN INTRICATE GLASS SCULPTURE BY DALE CHIHULY IS THE FOCAL
POINT OF AN ATRIUM AT SOUTHWESTERN MEDICAL SCHOOL,
LOCATED ADJACENT TO PARKLAND HOSPITAL AND CHILDREN'S

124

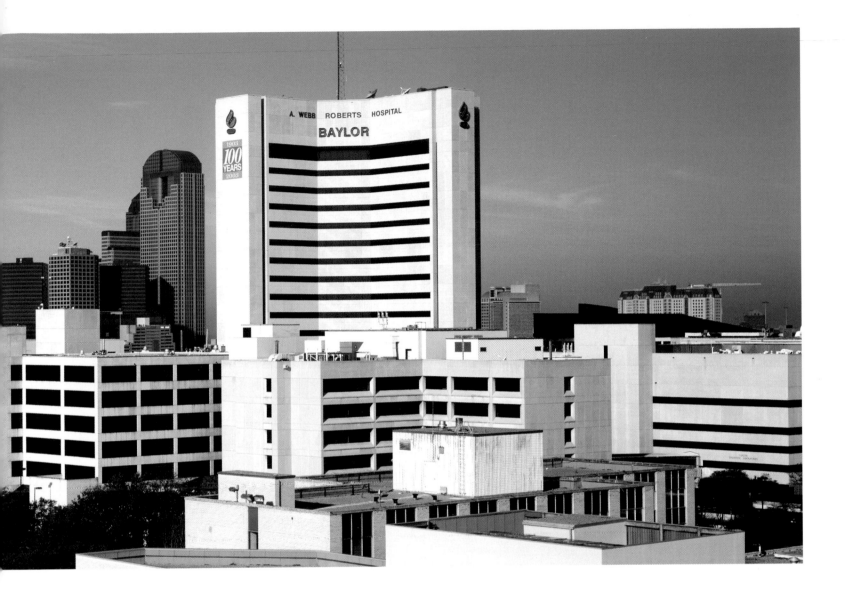

MEDICAL CENTER. FOUNDED IN 1943, THE SCHOOL BECAME PART OF THE UNIVERSITY OF TEXAS IN 1949 AND TODAY BOASTS FIVE NOBEL PRIZE LAUREATES ON ITS FACULTY. (LEFT) CREATED IN 1948 WITH THE MERGER OF FOUR EXISTING PEDIATRIC FACILITIES, CHILDREN'S MEDICAL CENTER HAS DEVELOPED INTO ONE OF THE LARGEST CHILDREN'S HOSPITALS IN THE NATION, PIONEERING NUMEROUS MEDICAL PROCEDURES.

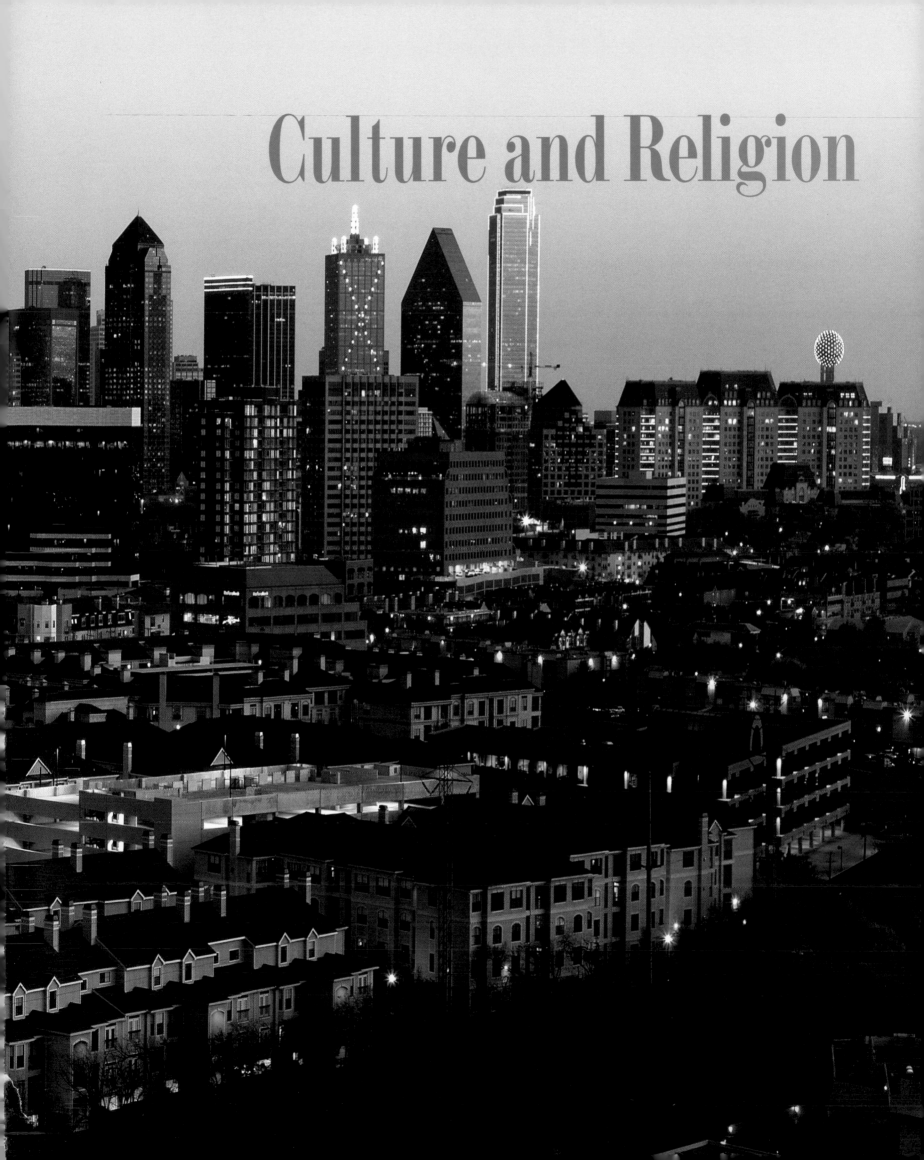

Culture and Religion

(OPPOSITE) RENOWNED TEXAS ARCHITECT NICHOLAS CLAYTON DESIGNED THIS GOTHIC REVIVAL CATHEDRAL FOR THE ROMAN CATHOLIC DIOCESE OF DALLAS. OPENED IN 1902, IT IS NOW KNOWN AS CATHEDRAL SANTUARIO DE GUADALUPE AND IS IN THE PROCESS OF UNDERGOING EXTENSIVE AND CAREFUL RESTORATION. (ABOVE LEFT) THE DEVOUT LIGHT CANDLES IN A SIDE CHAPEL OF CATHEDRAL SANTUARIO DE GUADALUPE BELOW A 100-YEAR-OLD STAINED GLASS WINDOW. (ABOVE RIGHT) THIS FIRED CERAMIC MURAL OF ST. ANNE WAS PAINTED IN THE STYLE OF EARLY MESO-AMERICAN MISSIONS AT THE HISTORIC ST. ANNE'S SCHOOL IN "LITTLE MEXICO" NORTH OF DOWNTOWN. ALTHOUGH MOST OF THE SCHOOL HAS BEEN DEMOLISHED TO MAKE WAY FOR NEW OFFICE CONSTRUCTION IN THIS DENSE URBAN AREA, PRESERVATIONISTS SUCCEEDED IN PRESERVING THE OLDEST PORTION OF THE SCHOOL, AND THE MURAL WILL BE PLACED FACING HARWOOD STREET, TO BE VIEWED FROM THE STREET.

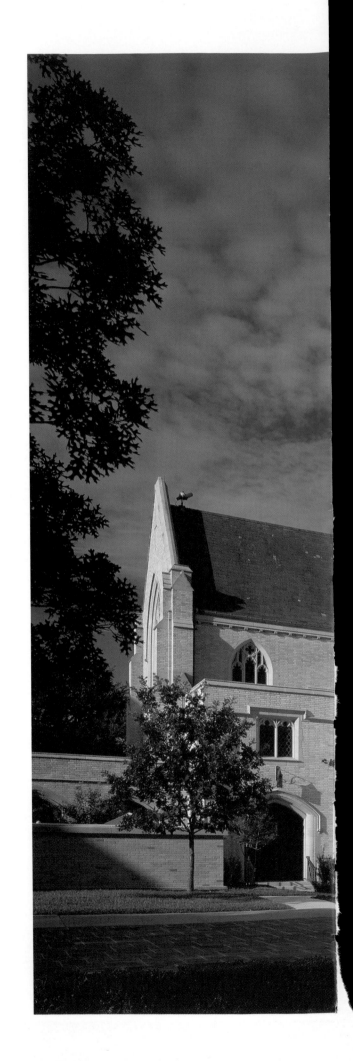

(ABOVE) STAINED GLASS WINDOW AT HIGHLAND PARK PRESBYTERIAN CHURCH. (PHOTO: COURTESY MEADOWS MUSEUM) (RIGHT) DALLAS ARCHITECT MARK LEMMON DESIGNED THE GOTHIC REVIVAL HIGHLAND PARK PRESBYTERIAN CHURCH IN 1929 AND ADDITIONAL BUILDINGS IN THE COMPLEX OVER THE NEXT FEW DECADES. AT ONE TIME HIGHLAND PARK PRESBYTERIAN WAS THE LARGEST PRESBYTERIAN CONGREGATION IN THE UNITED STATES. (PHOTO: COURTESY MEADOWS MUSEUM)

(OPPOSITE) ARCHITECT MARK LEMMON EMPLOYED ROMANESQUE DETAILS IN HIS DESIGN FOR THE THIRD CHURCH OF CHRIST, SCIENTIST, CONSTRUCTED IN 1931 ON OAK LAWN JUST SOUTH OF HIGHLAND PARK. (PHOTO: COURTESY MEADOWS MUSEUM) (THIS PAGE TOP) ALTAR: THIRD CHURCH OF CHRIST, SCIENTIST. (PHOTO: COURTESY MEADOWS MUSEUM) (THIS PAGE ABOVE) THE DALLAS CENTRAL MOSQUE IN RICHARDSON PROVIDES NOT ONLY A PLACE TO PRAY, BUT ALSO A SITE FOR EDUCATION AND SOCIAL SERVICES FOR THE REGION'S RAPIDLY GROWING ISLAMIC POPULATION.

(ABOVE LEFT) HORCHOW GARDEN AT TEMPLE EMANU-EL. (ABOVE RIGHT) IN 2000, THE CATHEDRAL OF HOPE CELEBRATED THIRTY YEARS OF SERVICE TO A PRIMARILY LESBIAN AND GAY CONGREGATION BY DEDICATING THE JOHN THOMAS BELL WALL. DESIGNED BY ARCHITECT PHILIP JOHNSON, THE TOWER HOLDS BELLS SYMBOLIZING REMEMBRANCE, JUSTICE, AND HOPE. (OPPOSITE) THE FIRST REFORM JEWISH CONGREGATION IN NORTH TEXAS, TEMPLE EMANU-EL WAS FOUNDED IN 1873. THE CONGREGATION MOVED INTO ITS THIRD HOME AT HILLCREST AND NORTHWEST HIGHWAY IN 1957. DESIGNED BY PROMINENT DALLAS ARCHITECT HOWARD MEYER, THE TEMPLE'S HEART IS THE SANCTUARY, ORNAMENTED BY GYORGY KEPE, MOSAIC-ENCRUSTED BRICK JOISTS AND ANNI ALBERS, ALTAR TAPESTRY.

(TOP) MEMBERS OF "CLEAN SOUTH DALLAS" HAVE ROLLED UP THEIR SHIRTSLEEVES TO RESTORE THE ORIGINAL BEAUTY OF THEIR HISTORIC NEIGHBORHOOD. (ABOVE LEFT) THE JUANITA CRAFT HOUSE IN SOUTH DALLAS DOCUMENTS THE INSPIRING CAREER OF ITS LONG-TIME RESIDENT, A CIVIL RIGHTS LEADER WHO ROSE FROM WORK AS A SEAMSTRESS TO ELECTION TO A SEAT ON THE DALLAS CITY COUNCIL. (ABOVE RIGHT) VISITORS TO OLD CITY PARK: THE HISTORICAL VILLAGE OF DALLAS ARE TRANSPORTED BACK TO A SIMPLER TIME WHEN THEY TOUR THE "SHOTGUN HOUSE", INTERPRETED AS THE HOME OF A WORKING-CLASS AFRICAN-AMERICAN FAMILY IN DALLAS

100 YEARS AGO. ORIGINALLY CONSTRUCTED IN 1906 ON GUILLOT STREET IN THE STATE-THOMAS NEIGHBORHOOD JUST NORTH OF DOWN-
TOWN, THIS WAS ONE OF TEN IDENTICAL HOUSES THAT STOOD IN A ROW. DEFINED AS A HOUSE THAT IS ONE ROOM WIDE AND AT LEAST
TWO ROOMS DEEP, THE "SHOTGUN" WAS SIMPLE AND INEXPENSIVE TO CONSTRUCT, AND IT'S ROOMS COULD SERVE MULTIPLE PURPOSES.
(ABOVE) FREEDMEN'S MEMORIAL PLAZA COMMEMORATES THE STRUGGLES OF FORMERLY ENSLAVED AFRICAN AMERICANS ON THE SITE
OF THE FIRST BLACK CEMETERY IN DALLAS.

(ABOVE AND LEFT) THE OPEN-AIR FARMERS' MARKET, ON THE EASTERN EDGE OF DOWNTOWN, HAS TEMPTED COOKS WITH FRESH PRODUCE FOR MORE THAN FIFTY YEARS. (FAR RIGHT) BETTY'S TOMATOES. LOCAL COOKS BUY RED AND JUICY TOMATOES AT THE FARMERS' MARKET.

Dallas: Where the Arts Live

Skyscrapers surround you—their lights illuminating the sky. The breeze of a warm summer evening. Hundreds of people enjoy an evening picnic on the museum lawn while swaying to the beat from the live jazz ensemble. The stained glass windows of the Cathedral Guadalupe reflect rainbows and prisms. The soothing sounds of waterfalls serve as a haven in the midst of the city. A serene place unites the sculpting mastery of Auguste Rodin, Pablo Picasso and Alberto Giacometti. Lights dim as a lone dancer glides effortlessly to music telling a story where no words are necessary. A multi-cultural festival at a square in the middle of the city brings together people to celebrate a culture several continents away.

Enthralled—caught up in the moment of a beautiful sensory experience in the middle of downtown Dallas?

Welcome to the Dallas Arts District, a place teeming with museums bringing together the great artists of the past and the up-and-coming artists of the future; masterful and cutting-edge dance performances ranging from classical ballet to contemporary modern dance; the architectural genius of I.M. Pei, Renzo Piano, Nicholas Clayton, Norman Foster, Rem Koolhaas; world-class musicians from the Dallas Symphony Orchestra; the stars of tomorrow from the Booker T. Washington School of Performing and Visual Arts. It is a kaleidoscope of sights and sounds and a tapestry of different cultures—all under the backdrop of downtown Dallas.

There is something here for everyone—music, art, culture, architecture, history, theater, preservation, dining, nightlife, sculpture, office towers, water gardens. Whether you experience the Dallas Arts District while the sun's rays shine on the oasis of landscapes and green spaces or when the sky is a canvas of stars twinkling in the moonlight—it is a place where commerce and culture intertwine like a fine, symphonic concert.

And there is a promise of more to come. The Dallas Center for the Performing Arts will serve as the future anchor for the city's arts organizations. State-of-the-art venues for Dallas' troupes of opera, ballet, theater and music will find a welcome home in the heart of the city. A multi-block area serves as an un-modeled piece of clay waiting to be formed into one of the undiscovered treasures of the art world. A reminder to all that Dallas is an international destination for the arts.

Experience art. Experience Dallas. Experience the Dallas Arts District.

Supporting this unique neighborhood is the Arts District Friends—a non-profit organization dedicated to championing and promoting the Arts District. The Arts District encompasses 17 blocks and 61.7 acres in downtown Dallas. For more information about the activities occurring in the District and the efforts of the Arts District Friends, visit www.artsdistrict.org.

(OPPOSITE) COLLABORATIONS BETWEEN THE NASHER SCULPTURE CENTER AND THE DALLAS SYMPHONY ORCHESTRA BEGAN IN OCTOBER 2002 WITH THE INSTALLATION OF *PROVERB* BY MARK SUVERO. THE 60-FOOT-HIGH RED STEEL SCULPTURE WAS INSTALLED ON THE LAWN NORTH OF THE MEYERSON SYMPHONY CENTER AT THE CORNER OF PEARL STREET AND WOODALL RODGERS FREEWAY.

DEDICATION

DALLAS: WHERE DREAMS COME TRUE IS DEDICATED TO THE VIBRANT, IMAGINATIVE PEOPLE OF
DALLAS, THE CITY WHERE DREAMS REALLY DO COME TRUE.

ACKNOWLEDGEMENTS

WITH THE EXPERT, DETAILED GUIDANCE AND NURTURING OF GARY CHASSMAN OF VERVE EDITIONS,
DALLAS: WHERE DREAMS COME TRUE EVOLVED FROM THE STUFF DREAMS ARE MADE OF TO AN ASTONISHING REALITY.

WITH THE PATIENCE AND IMAGINATION OF DESIGNER RANDELL PEARSON OF PEARSON DESIGN NYC,
WHAT WERE ONCE 'JUST PHOTOS' BECAME GORGEOUS SPREADS WITHIN A COLLECTION, MADE NEW WITH MEANING AND BEAUTY.

WITH THE ABUNDANT IDEAS AND EXUBERANT ENTHUSIASM OF JANE OFFENBACH,
MANY OTHERS WERE GATHERED INTO THE FASCINATING FOLD OF 'DREAMS'.

WITH THE KNOWLEDGEABLE PROFICIENCY OF MICHAEL V. HAZEL,
THE PHOTO CAPTIONS ADDED MUCH NEEDED BACKGROUND CONTEXT AND INFORMATION.

JIM DONOVAN'S BRAINCHILD, *DALLAS: SHINING STAR OF TEXAS*, LIVES ON THROUGH *DALLAS: WHERE DREAMS COME TRUE*.
JIM NAMED THE BOOK, IT WAS THE NAME HE WANTED FOR THE SHINING STAR BOOK IN 1994.

DALLAS IS A "SPORTS-CITY", AND WITH THE ADDITION OF INCREDIBLE SPORTS PHOTOGRAPHS OF MY MENTOR AND TEACHER,
MOSES OLMOS, THE SPORTS SECTION BECAME ONE OF THE STRONGEST CHAPTERS IN THE BOOK

IN THE EVER-FAITHFUL, ALWAYS-EXCELLENT PARTNERSHIP WITH BWC PHOTOLAB, UNDEVELOPED FILM BECAME REAL PHOTOS AND
REAL PHOTOS BECAME DIGITAL FILES. SPECIAL THANKS TO THE E-6 GUYS, GARY LOCKE, ED BACH AND CHUCK DROBENA.

HEARTFELT THANKS GO TO THE EIGHT GENEROUS ESSAYISTS, DOLORES BARZUNE, RICHARD BRETTELL,
WILLIAM B. LAWRENCE, MAYOR LAURA MILLER, RAY NASHER, R. GERALD TURNER, GAIL THOMAS, AND NANCY WILEY.
THEIR SCHOLARLY WORDS SET THIS BOOK APART FROM ANY OTHER.

LAST, BUT NOT LEAST, MY DEEPEST THANKS GO TO THE LOYAL AND LOVING SUPPORT OF JOHN LEVERANZ AND
OUR BEAUTIFUL DOG, LEON. IT WASN'T EASY LIVING WITH THE OVERWHELMING MASS OF PHOTOGRAPHS,
UNPREDICTABLE SCHEDULING AND THE ALWAYS DEMANDING NATURE OF A BOOK PROJECT.

LIBRARY OF CONGRESS CATALOGING-IN-PUBLICATION DATA APPLIED FOR.
ISBN 0-9660352-7-5
PRINTED IN ITALY

DESIGN BY RANDELL PEARSON, PEARSON DESIGN NYC
DEVELOPED AND PRODUCED BY VERVE EDITIONS, BURLINGTON, VERMONT
WWW.VERVEEDITIONS.COM

DISTRIBUTED IN THE UNITED STATES AND CANADA BY VERVE EDITIONS
VERVE@TOGETHER.NET

10 9 8 7 6 5 4 3 2 1

DALLAS: WHERE DREAMS COME TRUE IS AVAILABLE TO CORPORATIONS AND
OTHER RECOGNIZED ORGANIZATIONS FOR QUANTITY PURCHASE.
FOR INFORMATION PLEASE CONTACT: CEBPHOTO@SWBELL.NET
VISIT OUR WEBSITE: WWW.DALLASWHEREDREAMSCOMETRUE.COM